Once a Cowboy...

*Ride Hard,
Laugh often!*

Debra Coppinger Hill

alwaysConboy.net

Once a Cowboy…

A Collection of Cowboy Poetry & Stories

by Debra Coppinger Hill & Robert Beene

with photography by Angela Beene

Published by WestWord Press

A Division of Old Yellow Slicker Productions
In Cooperation with Lazy B Productions, Angela Beene Photography
and American Cowboy Company.

www.westwordpress.com or www.oldyellowslicker.com
www.lazybproduction.com or www.angelabeene.com
www.AmericanCowboyCompany.com

Selections in this book are featured on Debra Coppinger Hill's CDs *Common Sense, Men and Horses* and *Evening Cattle Calls...* and from *Cowboyology* by Robert Beene. For information on personal appearances or to purchase additional books, CDs or videos by Debra Coppinger Hill or Robert Beene or photography by Angela Beene, please contact:

WestWordPress / Old Yellow Slicker Productions
PO Box 348 ~ Chelsea, Oklahoma 74016 ~ 918-789-5288
oldyellowslicker@yahoo.com ~ www.oldyellowslicker.com

Printed in the USA by EC Printing.

ISBN-13
978-0-9797240-0-8

WestWord Press

In Honor Of
The Real Cowboys & Cowgirls
Of Our Past, Present & Future

And for Jeannie…Thanks for the Ride!

INDEX

INTRODUCTION
by Jeannie Sutton Hogue

Section One – COWBOYS

Section Two – COWGIRLS

Section Three – HORSES

Section Four – COWBOY FAITH

Section Five – LESSONS LEARNED

ACKNOWLEDGEMENTS
BIOGRAPHIES
and
RECOMMENDED SITES

Introduction

At the time I was introduced to Cowboy Poetry I had no idea what it was. As a writer I knew there were many types and forms of poetry, but as a whole it just didn't appeal to me. Then I was introduced to Cowboy Poetry through the works of Debra Coppinger Hill. I never thought I would come to love poetry as much as I now do, but once I read her poetry I understood something very basic; that she truly loved and understood horses as much as I do. Cowboy Poetry puts the reader on the writer's level. You become part of the poem.

Good Cowboy poetry touches the heart and fills the soul. It tells a complete story about Cowboys, Cowgirls, horses, cattle, the western lifestyle, the land and the struggles and joys of living in the American West. It leaves you emotionally involved and wanting more. Whether writing about the past, present or future of Cowboys and Cowgirls; Debra Coppinger Hill and Robert Beene draw the reader in and make them a part of the piece. Their personal understanding of the people and animals of the West is shared in such a way that we come away believing that we had the very experience we just read about. It is not unusual to come away with the heartfelt feeling that we too are Cowboys and Cowgirls.

This collection of Cowboy and Cowgirl poetry about real Cowboys and Cowgirls, by real Cowboys and Cowgirls is a gift of master word crafting. With two distinct styles (rancher and rodeo/farrier cowboy) Debra and Robert share a range of feelings from hysterical laughter to profound sorrow in their poetry. I found some pieces so inspiring that I quote them in my own books. (With permission of course!) With equally inspiring photographs by Western Photographer Angela Beene, this book is a classic example of real Cowboy Poetry.

In researching the origins of Cowboy poetry, we find that the cattle trails and the men who followed them in the late 1860's through the first of the 20th century are credited with creating this form. Stories told around a campfire by real Cowboys and repeated from cow-camp to cow-camp put in place an enduring legacy of literature.

How fortunate we are to be allowed to share the past and present traditions of the West through *Once A Cowboy*. So get your gear, saddle-up and follow along on the Cowboy trail as Debra Coppinger Hill and Robert Beene present Cowboy Poetry at its finest in this exceptional collection.

Jeannie Sutton Hogue

Equine Mystery Writer
The Jesse Statham Mystery Series

COWBOYS

Once a Cowboy...Always a Cowboy,
It's born into the blood,
It takes a man's true measure,
through rain-storm, wind and flood.

"I cannot explain why
anyone would want to be a cowboy;
but I do not understand anyone who wouldn't."

Robert Beene
Oklahoma
Cowboy, Poet, Singer and Songwriter.

Still Cowboys

The day is short and I have chores to do,
  No time to write but a line or two,
But please know this, when the day is through;
  In this world there still are Cowboys.

So if you wonder if we're still alive,
  As you work at your 'nine to five',
Just know this…we do survive;
  Because we are still Cowboys.

We're the ones, who wear no labels,
  As we work hard, doing what we're able,
To make sure you have food on your table;
  Yes, you can thank the Cowboys.

We're Men and Women, who still recall,
  Those Cowboys of yesterday who started it all,
Who pick up their companions when they fall;
  It's the creed of the Cowboys.

And just like in those Days of Old,
  We share our opinions and we get bold,
We may adjust, but we'll never fold;
  Because we are still Cowboys.

It's our choice and we're honored to be,
  Still riding the prairie from sea to sea,
Living in a country where we are free;
  To be Forever Cowboys.

Debra Coppinger Hill

You Just Never Know

"Don't laugh at him kid,"
Old Jim said to me,
"You just never know
what's there, that you can't see."

We were low on feed
and had come in to town,
When I saw this city feller
'bout half a block down.
An insurance salesman
dressed in boots and hat
He hadn't the look of a puncher
and was leanin' towards fat.

Then he saw me and Jim,
we're cowboy sure enough,
This city feller waved
and started for our truck.
I noticed a limp
as he headed our way
and a face that had seen
a lot of sun in its day.

Well they started talkin'
'bout things from the past
'Bout good horses and friends,
and how time went too fast.
I learned this feller
had cowboy'd for years
And as a bronc twister
he'd never shown fear.

He'd been an honest puncher
back when he rode for pay;
I wondered what he wouldn't give
for just one more day?

My respect he had gained
before he shook my hand,
Then gimped back to his office
leavin' me a better man.
As we drove back to the ranch
Jim told me the tale
Of his friend's misfortune
that took him off the trail.

"It was just dumb luck
It could happen to you or me"
His horse slipped, went down in the rocks
and shattered his friend's knee.
That busted knee had ended
that old Cowboy's career;
Since I first heard that story
it's been about fifteen years.

But truer words were never spoke
than the ones Jim said to me,
"You just never know
what's there, that you can't see."

Robert Beene

Birth of a Buckaroo

I was sittin' alone one evenin' after dark,
When outside the window the dogs started to bark.
I jumped from my chair and looked through the pane,
To see who'd be comin' this late up the lane.

I know'd who it was when I saw the old truck,
Was a young man from town, I think they called Buck.
He walked to the door and I let him right in.
"Jist come to see ya", he said with a grin.

His work was done and he'd run out of luck
With no where to stay 'cept his old truck.
He'd never worked cattle, but be willin' to learn'
And be a good hand if just given a turn.

Wouldn't ask for much and didn't need pay,
His main concern was a dry place to stay.
With spring comin' on and the rains we have here,
I figured some help would be nice to have near.

He asked 'bout the work; I told him get ready,
For hard work 'round cows, it stays pretty steady.
'Round cows he was green this young city feller;
But I'll tell ya for sure, Buck he weren't yeller.

We fed through the mornin' and he did his share,
And I'll tell ya by noon, we were hungry as bears.
The evenin' went fine; we were workin' horseback,
And I could tell before long the kid had a knack.

He'd never roped before, so I showed him how,
And it didn't take long to catch his first cow.
That summer went fast as most of them do,
But the truth was that Fall was way overdue.

Now Buck he learn't fast and saved most of his pay,
To buy his own kack and go his own way.
Winter was comin' and work would slow down,
But I talked to the boss 'bout keepin' him around.

Winter hit hard. It got colder'n hell,
Winds blew from the north and the temperature fell.
We fed every mornin' and chopped ice, too,
Then stopped to warm up with a hot cup of brew.

Buck never whimpered; no he'd never whine,
Like some city fellers I know'd in my time.
He stuck it out 'til the winter was through.
I'm tellin' ya boys, he'd become a real buckaroo.

He's still workin' horseback; I see him now and again,
He made a good hand, and a heck of a friend.
It just goes to show ya, Cowboyin's an art.
Ya don't have to be born one, for it to be in yer heart.

Robert Beene

Jake

He was just a stove-up old Cowboy
who only drank to ease the pain.
He really didn't need it except
when it was cold or gonna' rain.

He'd spent his life bull-ridin'
until he had that wreck.
The bull threw him high, he came down hard
and busted his leg all to heck.

He was my Daddy's best friend
until the day my Daddy died.
They had rodeo'd together;
at the funeral, he cried.

I'd see him every now and again
at one or another rodeo.
He always had kind words for me
and acted like he hated to see me go.

He gave me my first pony
and a saddle with a dally horn.
They say he drove my Mamma to town
the icy night that I was born.

I heard he'd talk about me
and only had good things to say.
He never told me to my face
but I knew that was just his way.

It came as a surprise to me
when I heard that he was dead.
I couldn't forget the last time I saw him
or the last thing he ever said;

"I wish you'd been my own son,
I'm proud to know you as a man.
I wanted to say 'I love ya'
while I'm sober, and I can."

Then he turned and strode off,
and his back seemed straight and strong.
I'm not real sure, but I'd have sworn
that limp of his was gone.

So, on those nights when I'm alone
and hurt gets in my way,
I think of him and the guts it took
to say what he had to say.

And now, when I see an old Cowboy,
a little drunk and broken down;
I stop and listen to the stories he tells
'cause I know he's been around.

And somewhere, Jake is bull-ridin',
hittin' in the eighties on every ride;
Young and free and wild again,
in that place called The Other Side.

Debra Coppinger Hill

**"It's not that you want to ride the bull,
it's just sometimes you have to."**

Duffy Moore ~ Cowboy

For Dad

He was my hero when I was a kid
And I trusted him in all that we did.
He taught me to ride and how to rope;
I remember his eyes all full of hope.

He was raising a cowboy and somehow he knew,
There's nothing in this world that I'd rather do.
We've rode together for work and for fun;
Whatever the chore, he's there 'til it's done.

"Work done right is worth more than the pay;
Whether building fence, snappin' broncs, or feedin' hay.
"Stand by what you say and always stand your ground.
Never start a fight, but don't ever back down."

He taught me a lot 'bout cowboyin' and such;
In some folks mind I don't amount to much.
But I'm cowboyin' now; some say I'm a top hand.
And if it's true, the credit goes to one man.

I've worked in the brush and out on the plains.
And I'll tell you for sure, I'm proud to have his name.

Robert Beene

Bitten

Cowboys don't fear the coyote,
   he just yips and yowls,
    But the wolf is another story,
    your blood chills when he howls.
And a panther, will stalk you,
   even in the dark,
    And a bear, when he catches you,
    will tear you clean apart.
The best thing about a snake bite,
   is it kills you pretty quick,
    And those "under a rock crawlies",
    their bite makes you deathly sick.
But the most vicious of the critters,
   the one every Cowboy fears,
    Inflicts a type of torture,
    that can leave grown men in tears.
With a bite so excruciating,
   it will make you wish that you were dead,
    And there's nothing more terrifying,
    than when it raises it's ugly head.
It attacks without warning,
   it's cold-hearted and just plain mean,
    It considers all men prey,
    and will bite any one that's seen.
The suffering, is lingering,
   and to this very day,
    There's no cure or medication,
    that can take the pain away.
It's just the size of a pin point,
   and it don't get much bigger,
    But I've seen Cowboys brought to their knees,
    by the savage bite, of the Chigger.

Debra Coppinger Hill

Good Old Boy

He pushed cattle up the trail
  one hundred years before we were born,
  but his legend lives on today.
And they called him Boy
  up to the moment he died
  but he was 80 if he was a day.

When he was young he rode
  from Texas to Cheyenne
  from the Yellowstone to the Rio Grande;
And he pointed them North
  headed for some cow town
  somewhere north of the Doan's.

And they killed his way of life
  with fences and the rail
  but he cowboyed on through those days;
And though age slowed him down
  he always stayed true
  to the cowboy he had always been.

They buried him deep
  in the west Texas sand
  far from any family he'd known;
And spoke kind words over him
  but they didn't understand
  this ole' Cowboy had finally gone home.

And he's riding again
  like he did when he was young
  with no fences across the trails;
And he'll cross Red River
  at the Doan's with his friends
  pushin' 'em north to the rails.

Robert Beene

Traditions

"Cowboyin's a thing of the past."
   That's what they all said
Back when I was a kid,
   With dreams fillin' my head.
No, cowboys weren't too popular
   In the towns where I grew up.
But, I've stayed true to my dreams
   Ever since I was a pup.

The trends would come and go.
   Sometimes "cowboy" would be in.
Then the styles would change,
   They'd just look at me and grin.
No, my style never changed
   Wranglers, boots, and a hat.
While they were wearing Gitano
   Or something else like that.

I'm not sayin' that they're wrong.
   To each his own, I believe.
But if they want me to conform,
   I'd be better off to just leave.

So here's to Tommy, and Brian,
   And all my rodeo friends
Who help keep rodeo alive,
   They don't adhere to the trends.
To Brewer and the Eslik brothers,
   They're still ridin' the range.
They're cowboys I tell ya,
   God knows they'll never change.

I've lived as a cowboy and I'll die the same;
And I thank the Lord, for my place in the game.

Robert Beene

The Last Cowboy

He's as wild as the wind
  on a west Texas plain,
And though many have seen him
  very few know his name.

A cowboy, a drifter,
  some say he's a saddle tramp;
But he's at his best
  punchin' cows at some line camp.

You don't now his name,
  and you can't feel his pain;
But most envy this horseback puncher
  'cause he still rides the range.

Sometimes you can see him
  from the highway at a distance;
Always horseback with his rope
  ridin' the endless fences.

He dreams of the days
  when there were no fences to ride,
When cowboys ran wild
  and the cattle ranged wide.

How the west was tamed
  with a rope and a gun;
Of the long cattle drives
  that end with the settin' sun.

Eight hundred a month
  and a room with a view;
His pay don't seem much
  to people like you.

But it pays for his snuff
  and the clothes on his back.
And once in awhile,
  he buys some new tack.

No, he don't have much,
  but he's earned all he's got;
So he'll stay out on the range
  or maybe some feed lot.

"A disappearing occupation"
  that's what they all say,
And he may never say it
  but he knows he's here to stay.

Robert Beene

Cowboy Attitude

I've seen a lot of tee-shirts lately,
that say "Get a Cowboy Attitude",
But the fellows who were wearing them,
appeared to be plain rude.

They think that being a Cowboy,
is a swagger in your walk,
And a dip in your lip,
and a drawl when you talk.

They think it means a high dollar horse,
and a trailer with a tack,
And a fifty-thousand dollar pick-up,
with vanity plates on the back.

They think a hundred dollar shirt,
and a Stetson with a fancy band,
Are all that it takes to make,
the measure of a man.

But being a Cowboy,
ain't necessarily what you ride,
It's what you believe,
it's who you are *inside*.

It's looking past the problems,
to further down the road,
It's standing up for others,
and living by *The Code*.

It's giving more than your share,
and doing what is right,
It's knowing how to appreciate things,
by taste, or feel, or sight.

It's knowing that it's not necessary,
to be Politically Correct,
That either you do, or you don't,
deserve your ounce of respect.

It's knowing the definition of Freedom,
the Responsibility that it brings,
It's Heart and Soul and Strength and Grit,
and even more than just those things...

It's wearing what is practical,
and even if you're money poor,
If you really are a Cowboy,
you're rich in Something More.

Because being a Cowboy,
isn't something that you learn,
It's putting your shoulder to it,
it's the one thing that you EARN.

So, when you see a fella',
wearing his "cowboy attitude",
You can know that he's a "wanna' be",
or maybe just a dude.

As for the Real Cowboy?
Well, you'll know him by the look in his eyes,
And he'll be the one wearing plain clothes,
'cause he don't have to advertise.

Debra Coppinger Hill

An Old Cowboy Friend

He's a cowboy at heart,
  a bronc-twistin' fool,
And he'd throw a rope on anything
  his old horse could pull.

He rode broncs and bulls
  back in his younger days,
But all the flash and glory
  is lost in a distant haze.

"Been married three times."
  he'll laugh if you ask;
But he won't talk
  'bout what's in his past.

"Women come and go," he says
  "Like the horses I have known,
But the latter is more faithful
  as experience and time have shown."

He's worked for the XIT,
  The King, and the 6666's;
He's doctored a lot of yearlings
  and rode miles of fences.

I worked with him last spring,
  he is a hell of a hand.
And wherever he is now
  you can bet, he's ridin' for the brand.

Robert Beene

A Little Reminder

He wears a three piece suit,
   and a bold silk "power tie",
But this weekday outer facade,
   is nothing but a lie.

'Cause inside, he's a Cowboy,
   and each morning as he rushes to feed,
He wishes he could drop that job in town,
   but it's not a matter of want , but one of need.

The job supports the family and the horses,
   but keeps him too busy to ride,
But he's a Cowboy for awhile each morning,
   at the barn, with the horses inside.

When he gets to his big meeting,
   he gets a small surprise,
And he hopes, for a moment, that what he sees,
   is seen only by his eyes.

Across the tail of his suit coat
   and up and across the lapel,
Is a stringy little reminder
   from a horse that loves him well.

An "I love you", written in mucus,
   and dried to a shine,
From the one who knows his heart,
   and who he really is inside.

Then it dawns on him, he's in a room,
   with men of money and of power,
And it's all he can do to keep from laughing,
   as he sits there for an hour.

You see, a little horse snot,
   can make you feel reflective,
And in certain circumstances,
   it puts the whole world in perspective.

Because you can be important,
   and wear silk with pockets filled with gold,
But you're still just somebody's "Bubba",
   when there's horse snot on your clothes.

Debra Coppinger Hill

One for Tommy

It was the fourth of July
in a rodeo town,
And all the home folks
were gathered 'round.

Some big names were there,
like Hedeman and Sharp;
But a young man named Trott
would prove he had heart.

With money he'd won,
his entry fees paid,
The dreams of a boy
were soon to be made.

He'd drawn a good bull
and was ready to ride,
Before he got through
that bull would lose hide.

This was the big time,
The P.R.C.A.;
Hoped to fill his permit
and take home some pay.

Just a slight of a man
couldn't weigh a hundred pounds;
But he'd ride like a pro,
when the bull come around.

He climbed in the chute,
and heated the tail,
Slid to his rope,
and prayed he'd not fail.

A nod for the gate,
and the bull starts out;
As they head for the sky,
the crowd starts to shout.

He turns to the left,
goes into a spin;
But Tommy starts spurrin'
and I saw a grin.

The whistle she blows,
Tommy steps to the ground;
Don't recall his mark,
but he won the round.

Gathered his pay,
Thanked God for his chance,
Packed his riggin' away,
and took one last glance.

His dream had come true,
he drove for the gate;
But this wouldn't be the last time,
this cowboy'd make eight.

Robert Beene

*"If I had a-just stuck him
one more jump an' a-rode him down,
well, then this a-here by God hole
would be full of somebody else!"*

Jeff Streeby from Sunday Creek

Self-Imposed Twilight

He sits beneath the light in the kitchen,
  on the table lay paper and pen,
He wants to write about old-time Cowboys,
  but he doesn't know where to begin.

"Follow close," a voice whispers softly,
  "Come and sit with us by the fire.
We'll tell you the tales of the men of the trail
  and the object of every Cowboy's desire.
In each Cowboy heart lies a wish,
  to be remembered for more than a night,
For the marks he made, the things he built,
  and for all the things he did right."

So he switches off the electric lights
  and as his eyes adjust to the dark,
He sees men and horses drifting in,
  gathering where a chuck-wagon's parked.
He lights an old lantern and joins them,
  these Cowboys of a time long gone,
With pencil and tablet he begins to write,
  as they laugh and ramble on.

The voices of these Cowboys carry him,
  drawing him ever deeper into the past,
"Tell our stories." they implore in a whisper,
  "Make us immortal, make history last."
Dashing down one word after another,
  across the paper his pencil quickly flies,
Making it real so others can see
  the world through a Cowboy's eyes.

It's his way of honoring them,
  sitting alone in self-imposed twilight,
Shutting away the modern-day world,
  listening and writing away the night.
In this darkness he sees things clearly,
  how their dreams and his intertwine,
Mixing with the smoke of the fire,
  bound as kindred spirits for all time.

Some snicker when he says he's a poet,
  they think it's not what a Cowboy should be,
But those who understand say he's also a prophet,
  preserving the past and future for you and me.
So he sits alone by the lantern,
  and writes because he knows he must,
The Spirits of the West have chosen him,
  and their stories to him entrust.

Taking down each account in detail,
  transcribing every word they say,
He writes until morning steals in
  and the sun melts the voices away.
"Safe journey my friends" he says softly,
  as they mount up and fade into the Blue,
"If the trail ever leads you back this way,
  please know I'm here waiting for you."

How I envy my friend this connection
  to those who lived our history,
And I am forever grateful
  that he shares their stories with me.
I yearn to be blessed with his vision,
  to see and hear clearly in the dark,
I hope one day he'll let me sit with him
  at a fire where a chuck-wagon is parked.

Debra Coppinger Hill

Regret

I've seen their spirits ride at night,
In total darkness and clear moonlight;
Souls that search for what is right,
These men that they call Cowboys.

With open heart, determined face,
Eyes that see a distant place;
No eternal rest 'til they run the race,
These men that they call Cowboys.

They search across history,
To return our civil gentility,
Back to the way things ought to be,
These men that they call Cowboys.

Nothing gets in their way,
Honor bound by what they say,
They pledge to bring it back one day,
These men that they call Cowboys.

Promise made, I over-hear,
From their mission, they'll not veer,
It's their duty to find the Lost Frontier,
These men that they call Cowboys.

I know their voices from my dreams
Calling me to come upstream;
Perhaps, my life, to redeem,
These men that they call Cowboys.

I must make haste and decide
If on this quest I will ride;
With them I know I can't backslide,
These men that they call Cowboys.

I pause...consider...hesitate...
They ride on, it is too late.
They leave me with my own mistake,
These men that they call Cowboys.

Waking, as if from a trance,
I cry out for one more chance;
But they have gone without a glance,
These men that they call Cowboys.

I realize they have come before,
Blazing trails, opening doors,
To Freedom, Salvation even more,
These men that they call Cowboys.

I know these men, I owe a debt,
I should have gone, it's my regret;
And to this day I seek them yet,
These men that they call Cowboys.

So I search for their spirits late at night,
In total darkness and clear moonlight;
And pray for the chance to set things right,
With these men that they call Cowboys.

Debra Coppinger Hill

"You crawl out of your bedroll
long before first light;
To the sounds of Cookie singing
and the campfire shining bright."

Tim Graham
Texas Cowboy Singer ~ From 'Saddling in the Dark'

COWGIRLS

**It knows no age or gender,
you receive just what you earn,
By stepping up, taking hold of the reins,
and never complaining about your turn.**

*"This is the life I dream of
as I drift off each night…
this place of tall grass and blue skies
where we ride hard and laugh often."*

*Debra Coppinger Hill
4 DH Ranch, Oklahoma,
Cherokee, Rancher, Poet & Columnist*

Old Yellow Slicker

She wears his yellow slicker,
  though it almost drags the ground,
It seems to make things easier,
  as if He is still around.

He's left her some big boots,
  she's gonna' have to fill,
But his old yellow slicker,
  seems to give her the Will.

The Will to keep on going,
  The Will to be wise and strong,
The Will to make their dreams come true,
  and remember, where she belongs.

She wears it to feed the cattle,
  and when she cleans the stalls;
She hangs it on that high nail by the door,
  and remembers He was tall.

She wears it every time,
  storm clouds come rushing in,
She even wears it sometimes,
  just so the tears will not begin.

She wears it to keep the wet out
  and to hold the cold at bay,
It eases the hardness of the ground,
  each time she kneels to pray.

She wears it to chop the tanks,
  and when she mends the fence,
She wears it on the best of days,
  and on the ones that make no sense.

She wears though it's ragged,
  and completely lost its charm,
Because if she's inside of it,
  she's back inside his arms.

It's just an old yellow slicker,
  but it's made her life complete,
It reminds her what's important,
  and it's kept her on her feet.

She's worn it across a lifetime,
  and she's never felt alone,
She's raised their kids, raised their cows,
  and she's made their farm a home.

And when she's gone, she tells the kids,
  "just hang it on that nail in the barn,
When you look at it, your hearts will know,
  His yellow slicker, saved the farm."

Debra Coppinger Hill

**"How do I make you understand
that this is HIS coat...this is My Jack's Coat."**

*Mrs. Oleta Nichols
Granbury, Texas*

* For Mrs. Oleta Nichols, Grand Lady of Texas

The Edge

"It will be a Long-day",
you would say, as you checked the cinch,
and with that I would know
not to expect you,
until darkness had begun.

Into the tall grass
you would ride.
And I, left here,
set the cabin straight,
and fed and watered and gathered eggs.

On the Long-days,
we lived in two worlds.
Yours, an open prairie covered in cattle.
Mine, a homestead covered in dust.

I often wondered
if the wind that so tormented me,
was the same wind
that you spoke of as magical.

I did not love this world then.
I loved only you.
And it was you,
and you alone,
who made it bearable.

On the Long-days,
knowing you would come back
tried, yet satisfied and pleased,
I wrote the letters to the family,
and lied about the love
I had for this place.

Then, you did not ride in.

They found the broken shell of you,
the horse dead too,
where you shot it to save it's suffering.
Never mind, that you suffered also.

Family and friends tell me
that this place is too much for me alone.
But I cannot...and will not, leave.

This place owes me your spirit.
And I will wait here,
until it comes in the wind
and pushes the dust away.

Until it picks me up,
and dances me across the prairie,
and into your arms;

At the edge of the darkness
where you ride,
at the end
of a Long-day.

Debra Coppingr Hill

Snakes in My Décolletage

When it's cold I dress in the height of rural western fashion in Carhart® insulated overalls and coat. Though my insulated underwear beneath might not match, I am totally coordinated in tan canvas as I make my way to the barn through mud and ice. As I go about the morning feeding of horses, cattle, goat, cats and dogs I consider myself fortunate to be living my life as a ranch woman.

I try to do my chores efficiently, using as few steps as possible and wasting little time. To save trips back to the barn I leave the shoulder straps of my overalls loose, forming a chest pocket into which I stick supplements, tools, etc. as I go about feeding the mares nearest the barn.

This morning I walked into the feed room, reached up and pulled down a square bale of hay. Stretching higher up for a second bale I pulled it towards me, tilting it against my chest for balance. It was early morning and it was dark...but not so dark that I couldn't see the bull snake on the other end of the bale. I started to step back to allow the bale to just fall when my legs encountered the previously dumped bale. I sat down with the second bale square against my chest. As the snake slid forward, I swear to you, not since Eve in the Garden had a snake smiled in such a mischievous way.

I am not afraid of snakes. I have a healthy respect for them; especially when I have a hoe or shovel in my hands. As I pushed the bale away the snake slid tail first into the "pocket" of my overalls. At this point I would like to tell you that I was calm and used lady-like language; however, that would be a bold-faced lie. Falling off the first bale onto my back I had a sudden flash of what it must be like to be a turtle. Thick, insulated clothes make it very hard for short, round women to get back up once they are in a prone position. Grabbing the wire of the bale, I managed to turn myself over and get to my feet. Once standing I began "the zipper dance". You know the steps...pull, tug, pull, stomp, pull, pull, pull!

I made my way out of the feed room and into the corral. Gathering my wits, I grasped the top of the zipper and the tongue and moved the zipper on the front of my overalls about halfway down. Unfortunately, this also loosened them at the waist and instead of falling out as I had hoped; Mr. Snake proceeded down into the left leg of the overalls, which fit me just snug enough that I could feel his every movement. Hope springs eternal when you are in a desperate situation; I figured he would go on down and would simply fall out the bottom of the leg of his insulated prison. That, was entirely too optimistic on my part. It was wet and muddy and I had pulled on my big rubber boots, with the bottoms of my overalls securely tucked inside.

As I danced about, my son came around the corner of the barn. Throwing myself onto my back in the muck of the corral I shouted, *"Quick, peel me out of these overalls! Snake! Snake! Snake!"* Kicking and struggling with the side zipper on the leg, I awaited his help; but he was no where to be seen! The mental image of a turtle on its back once again invaded my mind. As I screamed his name I saw him coming from the barn with a hoe and looking at the ground. "Where, Mom? Where?!" he kept asking.

"IN MY OVERALLS! GET ME OUT OF THESE!"

Grasping my boots he tossed them aside and began to tug at my overalls, which were still secured by their straps over my shoulders...inside my coat. I was grappling with the coat while my son dragged me around the muddy corral. I had the sudden realization that I *was* a turtle on its back and had the irrational thought "What would a turtle do?" (However, pulling my head in and ignoring the situation was not an option at this point.)

"COAT!" I screamed, *"OFF!"* Fortunately my son speaks fluent screech and was able to translate my cries into directions. Sitting me up, he jerked my coat off and returned to tugging at my overalls. With one industrious yank they came off and as they flew into the air, so did the snake.

I love old Roadrunner and Coyote cartoons, especially when impending disaster is played out in slow motion. This is the first time in my life that real time took on all the qualities of that poor Coyote having a boulder fall off a cliff onto him. The snake flew up, went into a stall, hung momentarily (still smiling, I assure you), curled into position, straightened out like an Olympic diver and propelled himself straight onto my stomach! My son, also in slow motion, watched the snake go up and down and made one comment, *"Duh-ang!"*

Rolling to one side I dumped the snake into the mud, grasped a panel, scrambled to my feet and grabbed the hoe. I would like to tell you again that I was very lady-like and magnanimous and that I allowed Mr. Snake to make his escape unscathed. This also, would be a lie. I do believe however, that when Mr. Snake got to reptile heaven he told the gatekeeper that he was dispatched from earth by a Marine Corp drill instructor wearing muddy long johns and socks. I will admit I may have over-reacted a teeny bit, as Mr. Snake vaguely resembled stir-fry when I was done.

My husband made it in from his latest job in the Gulf and went out to do the evening feeding. I had not related the day's events to him as I was in the shower for the second time that day. (More mud, a skittish bottle calf, you get the picture.) Fortunately for me, my son was with a friend and had not regaled his father with his version of this incedent. (Which differs slightly from mine…I did not pummel the snake with my fists nor did I shout, "This is for women everywhere!" Not that I recall anyway.)

As my husband came back into the house I heard him ask, "Who killed my snake?"

"What do you mean by *my snake,* Cowboy?" I asked in that unnerving controlled "mommy" voice that children and husbands fear.

Silence from the hall.

"You *knew,* it was there?" I asked. "And you *didn't* kill it?"

"Well, it eats mice and it never causes any trouble."

Wrong answer.

"It slid off a bale and *into my overalls.*"

More silence.

"I think I'll go back out and spend a little time in the barn before supper" he said as he retreated outdoors. *Smart man.*

There were lessons learned from this incident. I learned that children do listen to what we say. My son made me put seven dollars in the swear word fine jar for what he heard and told the whole county that his mother can kill a snake with lightning speed once it is outside her clothes. I learned that it doesn't matter if your long-john tops and bottoms match as mud co-ordinates everything into barnyard brown. I learned that my husband is pretty savvy when it comes to knowing when to make a quiet exit. I also learned not to repeat this story to friends or Jon will write a song about it.

The snake learned a valuable lesson too...Turtles, are tougher than they look.

Debra Coppinger Hill – Riding Drag

Dinner For One

On cold days
when the stock is gathered
near the tanks
and the steam rises from the water
and mixes with their breath
in the air,

She thinks of him
in that far away place
and wonders
if he ever thinks of her...

Then she spreads the feed,
scatters the hay
and talks to the horses,
Going on with this life
she was born to
and chooses to stay with.

But,
sometimes in the dusk,
as she drives back to the barn,
she hears his voice
saying he would give it all up
just for her,
if only she would say the word.

She supposes the word she said
was not the correct one.

She cannot
give up the land.

It will not let her.
It demands her attention.
And he is jealous,
but unwilling to fight
for her love.

So, she hangs up her coat,
kicks off her boots,
fixes dinner for one
and watches
the evening Ag. reports.

Before sleep
she will write in the farm journals
kept up for generations
and now her responsibility...
"Bred heifers looking well,
no sign of sickness,
water cleared of ice,
pump still working after repair."

She puts down her pen,
tucks herself in for the night,
and as she drifts to sleep,
she thinks of him;

And she wonders,
does he ever,
think of her...

Debra Coppinger Hill

One Question

A Cowgirl's work is never done,
endless chores keep her on the run,
Before the dawn, past the set of sun,
with no rest around the bend.
She never questions ranch-life's flow
or all the tasks that keep her on the go.
But there's one thing she wants to know...
"Hey...What's a week-end ?"

Debra Coppinger Hill ~/ 4DHRanch

Money For Her Diamond

In the heat of July,
  while bringing in the hay,
He gave her a baling wire ring,
  and this is what he had to say...

"Someday I'll put a diamond,
  here on your hand.
A diamond pure and perfect,
  as sure as I'm your man.

But, you know, a diamond,
  it won't ever shine,
As long or as bright,
  as this love of yours and mine."

So they saved for her diamond,
  by putting little bits away,
Money for the diamond,
  he would buy for her one day.

But the money for her diamond,
  fixed the tractor and bought a plow,
And in the dead of winter,
  paid the vet. bill for the cow.

The money for her diamond,
  put the water to the barn,
And paid the increased taxes,
  the county levied on the farm.

The money for her diamond,
  paid the doctor in town,
And when their daughters were all grown,
  it bought the wedding gowns.

It paid for the new roof,
  when the big wind came through.
Then it it paid off the mortgage,
  before it was due.

The money for her diamond,
  was always well spent,
She never even asked him,
  just where the money went.

The money for her diamond,
  helped them to survive,
The money for her diamond,
  kept their hopes and dreams alive.

Today it's been sixty-three years,
  and the diamond is on her hand.
But, as usual, in her pocket,
  lies her original wedding band.

A twist of baling wire,
  bent and covered up in rust,
A symbol of the greatest of loves,
  his Promise and Her Trust.

Debra Coppinger Hill

* For Ralph and Meekee for 64 years.

Stayin' Together

He didn't send her roses on Valentine's Day.
It's in February and he was still feedin' hay.

He forgot their anniversary for the last two years.
Last year he's pullin' calves and didn't see her tears.

Ah, she knows he loves her, but he's got a lot to do;
With taxes up and cattle down; it's got her worried too.

The first year was good; the ranch was payin' well;
But these last few years, she'll tell you, have been pure hell.

They barely paid the loan last year in December;
And last Christmas wasn't one to remember.

"We might lose the ranch." He 'bout cried when he said it,
But the man at the bank had said no more credit.

She knew it wouldn't be easy when she married a cowhand.
And nothing had turned out the way they had planned.

Cowboy'd for ten years before he bought this place;
Been free most of his life; now bankers stay on his case.

They still had six months to pay on the loan;
If prices held steady, they might hold their own.

But they'd stayed together through lots of hard times
And they'll be together, when they spend their last dime.

Robert Beene

Manure and Chantilly

The way she looked, I remember it well,
But even more, I remember the smell.

She'd fix her hair and lipstick,
  put on a chambray shirt and jeans,
It was the same thing every morning,
  the most familiar of scenes.
Then she'd do the one thing,
  that gave her the sparkle of a young filly,
She'd open that big round bottle,
  and sprinkle on Chantilly.

To us, it was wasted effort,
  after all, she was headed out to farm,
At the end of the day she'd be covered,
  with all kinds of manure from the barn.
But, one day when the work was over,
  and the evening meal was set,
Her husband said something,
  that is inside my mind yet...

He watched her as she cooked,
  took a deep breath as she sashayed by,
Grinned and said " Don't she smell sweet, like work?"
  as a twinkle came to his eyes.
Suddenly I understood,
  what made her efforts all worthwhile,
She had done it for Him,
  and that broad, loving smile.

It changed my entire outlook and you might think it's silly,
There's something about the smell, of manure and Chantilly.

Debra Coppinger Hill

Cow Tag

Most of the time I'm in a truck when I'm among the cows and calves, it's just easier to check them that way. But sometimes I feel the need to walk through the pastures and to be in closer contact. Since the evil Brahman cow Lucille is no longer with us, I have little fear, though I am cautious. I'm only five foot one and I don't stack up very well against a full grown cow.

We're starting to wean and in an effort to expedite things I took a walk into the pasture to look things over and to make some mental notes. Enter Mud Pie. She was my daughter's project last year, a bucket calf, which turned out nice enough that we kept her as a replacement. Our only problem with her is her personality. Unlike Lucille who viewed everyone and everything as a target, Mud Pie is friendly… excessively friendly.

On my trek across the pasture I kept my distance and tried to appear aloof. I didn't want the cattle to get the idea that I had any intention of chasing them or feeding them. Checking off cows and their calves in my head, I had a pretty good idea who needed to be separated and who should be tagged and moved to the other pasture. I was nearly done and was making my way back beside the small creek when I heard hoof-falls coming up quickly behind. Mud Pie had spotted me and apparently thought since a person was in the pasture that there must be a snack involved. This is the down-side of bucket calves. They get attached to humans and if you have a soft-hearted daughter who sneaks cubes to them as a treat, they get the idea that all two footed creatures mean one thing…food.

As a general rule, I'm pretty quick on my feet. To avoid getting run down, I dodged behind a pecan tree on the edge of the creek. Mud pie followed in hot pursuit as I moved from one tree to the next along the creek bank. I may have failed to mention that I have a broken bone in my foot and my balance is a little precarious at this time. I didn't want my foot stepped on and further damage caused, so I kept gimping along from one tree to another, with Mud Pie dancing around the tree-trunks after me like two kids playing a game..

It is thirty yards to the barn gate from the last tree. Being slightly injured played against me as I dash-hopped towards the safety of the west corral. Mud Pie caught up to me, put her head against my back pockets and lifted me into the air. I landed on my feet about a yard and a half in front of her. Cringing, I steeled myself for another flight. At that moment I heard my daughter's voice sing out "Muuud Piiie! Heeere Girrrl!" Mud Pie slid to a stop, veered to the left and headed for her owner. I limped towards the gate, secured it behind me and stood and watched as my daughter fed the villain a handful of alfalfa cubes.

I have raised my kids to listen to me when I talk to them. I expect them to remember what I say and to follow my directions. It's good to hear one of them repeat something that I have said; it makes me feel as if they have listened and learned. As I caught my breath, my daughter turned to me and in an un-amused-mother tone said, "I wish you wouldn't play tag with her like that, it makes her think she can do it with anyone." I started to talk back, but if memory serves me, she didn't talk back to me when I told her that very thing last year when Mud Pie was small. It's true what they say, "What goes around, comes around." My words have come back to haunt me and tag, I'm it.

Debra Coppinger Hill – Riding Drag

The One True Love

He was just a cowboy that worked out on the plains.
  He never had been married; no son to leave his name.
He was in love one time; he thinks of her now and then,
  And wonders to himself just how it might have been.

She was pretty as a picture, with a figure hard to beat.
  He recalls her confirmation; so refined, proper, and neat.
Her grace was overflowing, as noticed as her beauty;
  To defend her from all harm was his solemn sworn duty.

He'd ride through hell and back if only she'd request;
  No other woman on this earth had the beauty she possessed.
Many times he rode through storms in the night,
  Just to see her briefly in the early mornin' light.

She lived at the edge of town out in New Mexico.
  He still remembers her fondly; but that's been years ago.
He really should have asked her to marry at the time,
  But he was just a cowboy and didn't have a dime.

Oh, he thought about askin' but he never come to taw;
  'Cause if the truth be known, she didn't know him at all!

Robert Beene

**"If I can't go out to my truck any time in my
underwear, somebody lives too close."**

Leigh Ann Matthews
Singer, Songwriter and Publisher

Home-work

I didn't do the dishes, but in the first light of the morn,
I stood silently by a mare and watched her foal be born.

I didn't do the laundry and I didn't make the bed,
I shoveled stalls and fed calves as the sun rose crimson red.

I didn't clean the windows or take the time to dust,
I sorted baby chickens and replaced fencing that had rust.

I didn't sew or mend and I didn't sweep the floor,
But the things I did make this place a home and even more...

I use my heart and hands helping creatures give new life,
And elevate my status, to the title "Rancher's-wife".

If you can stand the inside mess, you're most welcome here,
To enjoy my home, outside and the wonders of God so near.

Debra Coppinger Hill

"My heart begs for freedom;
my spirit will not be tied.
I want all that I dream of,
my destiny, un-denied.

It's not just the land,
for which many pay a high price.
I'm not talking about a dollar,
I'm talking about a life."

Emily Richardson / BarCPublishing.com

Pretty Shoes

I used to wear pretty shoes,
now I just wear boots,
'Cause my family and Mother Nature,
are surely in cahoots.

They take me to places,
that are ankle deep in mud,
And those pretty, dressy shoes,
are soon filled with crud.

So I no longer paint my toe nails,
and I'm a complete stranger to hose,
I'm just a cow country female,
who wears boots where-ever she goes.

Debra Coppinger Hill

Ranch Kid Melody

Our music department gets very little money from the school budget. Most of the funds come from the parents support group and from a spaghetti dinner held each year. The food is donated and Chelsea Jazz Band provides entertainment. It's the band kids I want to brag about. Practice is done before school. The kids come on their own time in order to be a part of the band. "So what", you may think "an hour before school is no big deal." It is a big deal. Predominantly farm and ranch kids, an hour before school for practice also sets the time they get up to do chores back an hour or more.

The modern world may have changed most teen-agers, but rural kids are different. They have a sense of responsibility that most kids do not. Their chores contribute directly or indirectly to the economy of the family farm or ranch and they accept that. Yes, we have some complaints; they are teen-agers, after-all; but as a general rule, they take care of business before (and after) pleasure.

My daughter plays saxophone in the Jazz band. Each summer she attends camp at Jazz on the River an hour away. In spite of all the extra work and time she must spend in order to take part in band, she never misses doing her chores. She gets up at 5:30 a.m. or before to feed her horses, dogs and cats, check water tanks and care of her FFA steers. She repeats the process when she comes home from school.

The band concerts draw more than just the usual family members. It's the best show in town and it's free. The community looks forward to the presentations. People with no kids in school come to listen and enjoy the music. It has become such a culturally significant gathering that local and state politicians have begun to show up just to be seen there.

At this year's final concert the Jazz band played the last time slot. They looked great, dressed in their best outfits like the pros they are. After several encores the concert ended, but the band members stayed another two hours putting away chairs, cleaning and hauling instruments back to the band room blocks away. Then they got to go home to enjoy the compliments of their families.

My daughter wore a lovely long skirt, lace blouse and heels. It did my heart good to see her out of her usual blue jeans and farm equipment tee-shirt. I was waiting when she came home, ready to tell her how wonderful her solo sounded and how much I enjoyed hearing her play. She stepped inside the door, kicked off her heels, slid her mud-boots on and said, *"Hang on Mom, I'll be right back."* Half an hour later she was still outside. As I walked up to the barn I heard her voice talking low to her old, very pregnant mare.

She stood there in her lady-like skirt, blouse and her very utility-like mud boots rubbing the mare's belly. She was telling her that everything would be all right, the new baby would get here soon and that she would personally make sure the mare was not alone. I'd spent the evening being proud of my daughter as a musician and thought nothing else could happen on this day that would top the concert. But there she stood, a musician, with every reason to be reveling in her glory; taking responsibility once again without being told. A Ranch Kid with talent in more ways than one.

I asked her, *"Don't you want to go inside and change?"*

"Aw Mom, it's ok, Gypsy needs me. I'll change later."

And that, my good friends, is music to my ears.

Debra Coppinger Hill – Riding Drag

ll

*The colt's name is Gypsy Mellow D, in honor of our Musician Rancher.

The Dream

I used to cowboy for a livin'
  but now I work for the state.
Don't get me wrong, it's a good job,
  but I never believed it my fate.
Well, I'm older now,
  responsibility is mine;
With a wife and two boys,
  cowboy wages left us in a bind.

So I dream of the days
  when I was young and wild,
With no worries but me,
  no more burden than a child.
Sometimes it gets tough,
  and I think I'll chunk it all;
The bills, the debt, the worry,
  without it I'd have a ball.

Not too long ago
  I was feelin' boxed in,
And bein' a pain
  in my wife's cute rear end.
I grumbled about my job,
  the confines of our land;
Then one night while sleepin'
  God took me by the hand.

He gave me a dream
  I dreamed since just a boy;
Pushin' cattle up the trail,
  my heart filled up with joy.

The plains were so flat,
  and the sky was so clear;
You could see for days
  over your horse's ears.

The cattle were movin'
  at a nice easy pace;
As I looked around,
  I knew every man's face.
Most of them were friends
  I'd known since a child;
Looking over the herd,
  I felt myself smile.

One steer doubled back
  headed west at full stride;
But my pony was quick,
  and was after his hide.
The loop that I throwed
  was the prettiest I'd seen;
It slipped through the air
  'round his horns real nice and clean.

In one smooth move,
  popped my slack over his hip;
My pony cut hard,
  we turned that steer a flip.
Well that's how it was,
  at least in my dream;
We pointed them north
  a drifting cattle stream.

We came to Doan's crossing
  along about mid-day
And crossed the bloody Red,
  no toll of life did we pay.

Each night we'd bed down,
  the night guards would sing
And once in awhile
  a coyote's answer would ring.

As I lay on my bedroll
  picking out each sound;
I couldn't help but notice,
  I was feelin' awful down.
Though all my friends were here
  and the drive was going well,
I realized something was wrong,
  my heart was tryin' to tell.

How something was missing
  in this perfect dream I had
And how my real life
  wasn't really all that bad.
I turned in my bedroll
  and into sleep I drifted;
Then something happened,
  and my spirit was lifted.

I woke with a start,
  my eyes open wide,
For I felt my wife sleepin'
  right there by my side.
I knew I wouldn't trade her
  for the dream in my head.
'Cause she's a gift from God
  layin' next to me in bed.

Robert Beene

Dust Devil Waltz

I lean against the porch rail, look out across the land,
  Brush back unruly hair with a tanned and weary hand;
As the dust begins to roll I breathe a prayer for rain
  And listen for the sound of his spurs ringing again.

I dance with tumble-weeds, pretend we're not apart,
  Dream of far off places & the man who holds my heart;
On the wind I hear his words of magic filled with rhyme
  And I know he's out there dancing on the embers of time.

I keep this place together and I am not afraid,
  I've memories, a home and the promises he made;
Clean the dust from the windows and wait for my chance
  To ride the wind into his arms, once more to dance.

Dust devil swirl, across the wide prairie
Dust devil dance a wild waltz with me
Twirl me to him, he's waiting I know
Prairie breeze…tumbleweed…dust devil blow…

And listening with my heart I hear him singing low,
Prairie breeze…tumbleweed…dust devil blow…

Debra Coppinger Hill

* Dust Devil Waltz appears on the CD *Embers of Time* with music and
arrangement by Jean Prescott.

*"The days all run together
but I really can't say I mind,
For my time among the horses
is the most peaceful that I find."*

*Debra Coppinger Hll
4DH Ranch*

Wild Stick Horse Remuda

Ponytails and blue jeans,
  sat at Papaw's knee,
Watching as he whittled
  on old branches from a tree.
And while he talked of Cowboys
  and big old Texas ranches,
He trimmed away the rough spots,
  while I dreamed of pony dances.

A wild stick horse remuda
  began to run and play,
With every loving stroke,
  as he peeled the bark away.
Using his "Old Timer"
  and carving in my brand,
The best that he could find
  and cut and shape with his own hand.

Now, each one of them was special,
  and I felt I was too,
As they kicked up dust behind
  this cowgirl buckaroo.
With reins of pink hair ribbon,
  shoe strings and baling twine,
There was *Buckin' Birch*, Oakie
  and *Ole Sticky* made of pine,

Sassafras and *Blackjack,*
  Willow, Blaze and *Scat,*
I never did corral 'em --
  I just left 'em where they sat.

But next mornin', by the front porch,
  'stead of roamin' wild and free,
They'd found their hitchin' rail,
  'cause Papaw lined 'em up for me.

Along our trails together
  there were many lessons learned,
Like bein' a cowboy through and through
  is something that you earn
We'd partner up together,
  and team up in cahoots,
Once he defied my Mama,
  bought me red Cowboy boots.

And often, when I wondered
  what to do on down life's road;
He'd always tell me, "Little girl,
  when you get there you'll know,"
Sometimes you have to let things go,
  sometimes you stand and fight,
And anything worth doin',
  is still worth doin' right.

With my wild stick horse remuda,
  we rode the range for miles,
I knew I'd won my Papaw's heart
  by the way he'd laugh and smile,
I still have his sweat-stained Stetson,
  his boots and his old knife;
Sometimes I take them out
  just to measure up my life.

I hold him closer to my heart,
  and know I have to try,
To live up to the honor
  of those wonder-days gone by.
On my stick horse remuda,
  I learned the Cowboy way.
I'd give up everything I own
  Just to ride with him today.

My wild stick horse remuda
  was quite the varied band,
Born and bred with me in mind
  and trained by his own hand.
I'm longing for the legends,
  and the way we used to roam,
With my wild stick horse remuda,
    and the man that we called "Home".

Debra Coppinger Hill
Arrangement and music by Devon Dawson

* *In loving memory of my Papaw Ralph Gass who taught me to whittle and who gave me my love of the west. This piece appears on Debra's CD Common Sense, Men and Horses and the Devon Dawson CD 'Keepin' Your Head Above The Water'.*

HORSES

It's a sacred eternal connection,
as man and horse meet eye to eye,
And our spirits experience freedom,
as we break loose and fly.

*"I thank God every day for horses
and the healing power He sends through them."*

Jeannie Sutton Hogue
Georgia
Equine Mystery Writer

Listen

When the horses talk to me,
They tell me many things,
Whats and hows of yesterday,
Why the nighthawk sings.

I learn the meaning of the dance,
Between animals and men;
They inspire me to take the chance,
To look back on where I've been.

On this plain where we live,
In the circle at the center,
You receive more than you give,
When privileged to enter.

So I close my eyes in trust and walk,
And listen, to the horses talk.

Debra Coppinger Hill

*"The Call of the Wild sings straight to our souls;
To watch horses running is magic to behold!"*

*Jen D. Enise
Cowboys-n-Cowgirls.com
From Spirits Enchanting*

MUSTANGS

I went to work for him that year,
  early on, in the fall,
It was my job to help feed,
  water, and clean the stalls.

The quarter horses that he raised,
  were among the finest to be seen.
Then there were the mustangs,
  rough and rank and mean.

From time to time, the mustangs,
  would somehow make an escape,
No matter how carefully it was chained,
  they seemed to be able to open the gate.

Then we'd saddle-up and chase 'em,
  and push 'em back to the pens,
When it came to the mustangs,
  trouble knew no end.

He never really answered,
  when I asked him why,
He kept these three, who were dangerous,
  with such wildness in their eyes.

Once, he said, "They're the last of our kind,
  a rare and special breed,
Spirits, not of this earth,
  waiting to be freed."

This didn't help me understand,
  the mustangs or this man,
Who seemed to keep them at all costs,
  though they didn't wear his brand.

Then one day as we fed, I saw him...
  as He took loose the chain...
Softly, he said, "Come with me",
  and we walked to the truck in the rain.

We rode that old truck up to the hill,
  where we could see for miles.
Motioning to the tailgate, he bade me sit,
  and gave me a knowing smile.

Below, the mustangs had finished their feed,
  and as if they had good sense,
They began their morning journey,
  around their pasture, checking fence.

When they came to the gate,
  for a moment, they did pause,
And gave a glance towards the hill,
  as if they knew the cause.

I will remember the next few moments,
  Forever, they are etched into my mind,
And the emotion I felt, as we sat in silence,
  never again, shall I find.

We watched them bolt from the gate,
  Running for all they were worth,
All four feet up off the ground,
  Flying, between Heaven and Earth.

The explanation that he gave,
  he didn't have to give;
But, his words ring in my memory,
  all the days that I live.

He said, "I let them go sometimes,
  so I can remember, when I see,
What it's like to break loose,
  and truly, be Free.

For awhile I'm allowed, by Grace of God,
  to be a part of wondrous, unseen forces...
And that, my fine young friend,
  is why I keep wild horses."

Debra Coppinger Hill

The Little Roan Mare

I know you've heard the story 'bout a strawberry roan,
　of how he threw a bronc-twister and rattled his bones.
But this story is true...Yes, every part,
　I was workin' up north, perfectin' an art.

Now the boss was a drunkard and that ain't no lie,
　he'd get drunk and buy things; it helped keep him high.
He bought a roan mare from a ranch I won't name;
　"Do anything on her." Workin' cows was her game.

Now she was bred for it and had lots of heart,
　but as for workin' cows, she wanted no part.
The boss was still drunk and believed what they'd said,
　'bout "how she'd work cows until she was dead."

I knew what would happen when I threw on my kack
　and prayed to the Lord I'd stay on her back.
I stepped into the saddle and felt her back bow,
　sat quick in the wood waitin' fer her to blow.

She swallows her head and jumps for the clouds,
　I'm still in the saddle and feelin' mighty proud.
She's slingin' her head, kickin' her hind feet,
　but I knowed sure 'nuff that I had her beat.

Cowboys were whoopin' and throwin' hats in the air.
　I went to spurrin', the air filled with hair.
I felt her weaken and knew I had won,
　then saw where she's headed and thought I'z done.

She's runnin' full stride with me sawin' the bit,
　I kicked from the stirrups just 'fore we hit.
Two braces shattered as we busted through the wood;
　windmill crashed, Cowboys hid where they could.

The roan mare was down but she'd be okay,
  I weren't so lucky, I'd be hurtin' fer days.
With four busted ribs, I lay on the ground
  they were all laughin' as they gathered 'round.

I got to my feet and caught that roan mare,
  stepped into the saddle and said a short prayer.
A bronc-twister I'm not, though I ride pretty good;
  with the help of the Lord, I'll stay in the wood.

Robert Beene

*"I can be having the worst day, but when I go out to
the pasture and the horses gather around me and I
touch them; I can feel all the tension drain out of me
and be replaced with peace."*

David Hill
4DH Ranch

That Moment

He said "I can't explain it,
there are no words of course,
For that moment when you're training
when you truly connect with the horse.

Everything comes together,
it sets your soul to reeling,
You either get it or you don't,
it's an indescribable feeling.

So call it Swapping Spirits,
'cause nothing can compare,
To when you are the horse and the horse is you,
and you're breathing the same air.

Debra Coppinger Hill

Horseback Hymn

There's a certainty within us all
that tells us we should ride,
And give our hearts to the West,
our feelings we'll not hide.

There's a sanctity of the Spirit,
in the movement of the wind,
And a peacefulness from the soul,
that comes from the Earth within.

There's a silence in the moment,
that fills our hearts with glee,
And an openness to the light
that sets our Spirits free.

There's a gift of Salvation
when we throw our arms out wide,
When we look to the certainty
that tells us we should ride.

Debra Coppinger Hill

*"Horses are the best kind of friends. They're always
there when you need them and all they want is you."*

*Dara Hill
4DH Ranch & FFA Secretary*

Spirits Pure

I could not see them
  but I knew that they were comin',
The Earth shuddered with their cadence
  'til it shook my very soul,
As I lay there safe in hiding
  up along the ridge,
Strange whispered callings
  beckoned me to go.

From the ledge the valley floor
  stretched out before me,
As I stood entranced
  my blood raced with the wind,
Our life-breath joined as one
  as they galloped into view,
Wild hearts and hoof-beats
  charged around the bend.

I could smell their sweat
  as it poured out of their bodies,
Horsehide shimmering like
  crystal as they raced into the sun,
It took no words to teach
  the message or the meaning,
I saw freedom, love
  and truth on the run.

Mother Earth rose up to greet me
  as they ran at their full power,
Hoof-strikes set the dust to swirlin' clouds
  that billowed toward the sky,

My heart beat wild within my breast
  to the tempo of their thunder,
It filled me with joy ... for with them...
  I could fly.

I can still feel all around me
  the wonder and the splendor,
That stole my breath
  as they came into sight,
And the vision that reached out to me
  that day above the valley,
Is the dream I dream
  as I drift off each night.

It's carved upon my heart
  and on my memory,
Spirits wild and pure
  at one with Mother Earth,
I found my freedom there
  within those magic moments,
Their strength infused my soul
  with the glory of rebirth.

Now some say to reach for Heaven
  your soul must journey far,
To where the streets are paved
  with gold and precious pearls,
But for me it's on a ridgeline
  high above that endless valley,
At one with the horses
  at the top of the world.

*Debra Coppinger Hill & Jen D.Enise. Music, Arrangement and
Additional Lyrics by Jon Messenger and appears on his CD Spirits.*

Where the Horses Pray

I follow the trail of hoof-prints
  stamped deep in the snow,
And keep my own footsteps
  in line with where they go.
Their hooves pack down the trail,
  easing my journey as I creep,
Across the pasture I track them,
  through the brush and along the creek.

The horses know I'm there
  and so they lead me on,
Across a landscape of diamonds
  until we reach the deepest pond.

They stand at the edge,
  paw away ice and bow to drink,
And in a lightning-split moment,
  with no time to stop or think,
They raise their heads and their breath
  steams forth and hangs in the air,
Swirls around and mixes with mine,
  and rises high in prayer.

I have stood on the tops of mountains,
  I have sailed on the bottomless sea,
But here, on this expanse of prairie,
  is where He comes to me.

He sends His angels as Horses,
  strong and quick and sleek,
To guide me in my worldly quest,
  and help me find that which I seek.
As guardians of my spirit,
  they reveal without a word,
That even without speaking,
  our every prayer is heard.

So you can laugh and think I'm odd,
  but when I stand on snow-covered sod,
Where the hearts of untold Horses trod,
  I know I'm seeing the face of God.

I could preach for a life-time,
  and never fully explain,
How I know that it is He
  who goes by many names;
Who leads me to still waters
  along the Horses' trail,
And lets me know without a sound
  that His love will never fail.

Take my hand and follow,
  share the glory of this snow-bound day,
I'll show you a trail of hoof-prints,
  and the place where the Horses pray.

                    Debra Coppinger Hill

The Last to Sell

I thought from out here I wouldn't be able to hear the sounds of the auctioneer and the clacking of his hammer. The rolling echo of numbers trilling from his mouth bounces across the hills that surround the ranch. I'd like to say that this is the end of it all, but I know it's just the beginning. After the sale there will still be the bits and pieces to dispose of…a broken piece of equipment that no one would take, a stray cow or two who eluded the roundup and a horse too old and too much of a pet for the sale ring. Today is the easy part; "tighten up, sign the papers and put them in the auctioneer's hands." Tomorrow the real work begins.

If you wanted to put your finger on the very moment that it all went wrong, you would search forever. There is no one moment in ranching that can be defined as a turning point. Moments meld together to form life as a whole. It is up to us to take what's left and start over, time and time again. It's a part of the circle that we are all participants in. Life ebbs and flows, the market goes up and down and all the while, time just keeps on spinning.

As a child I always felt safe. Day to day we fought the elements, boredom, the bank and the baser instincts of livestock. Papa was our anchor; always pulling things together when we were scattered. I figured he would live forever and I lived my life according to his rules; which were always flexible when it came to me. My days were filled with endless adventures, usually involving one horse or another. My favorite, a big hipped bay mare with short white socks in back, carried me a thousand miles as I chased imaginary outlaws, rode as parade queen and won the Best All Around buckle in my wild dream rodeos.

Funny, how when we are kids we never see the problems of the adults around us. Late at night I would awaken to the sounds of pen scratching on paper and I would slip down the hall and venture a peek through the door to the kitchen. Papa would be at the table, lamp and papers before him, making entries in the ranch journals and figuring accounts. Never did he look as solemn as he did at those times. "We'll just have to tighten down some," he would tell Mama, "sell off the cows and horses; all except the bay, she can help out...she will be the last to sell." He would go back to figuring as I silently tip-toed back to bed and sleep; my world secure.

After selling off, he would tell us 'if a man has just one good horse, he can always make a living'. Bay would be brought into service as Papa did outside jobs working cattle and shoeing horses on neighboring ranches. I would often go with him. Riding along behind, my arms around him, I listened as he whistled and told me how starting over is a gift from God and always a good thing because it gives us new things to look forward to. While he shoed horses for the neighbors, I rode Bay and never missed out on adventure.

Time makes changes that we have no control over. Like Papa, I took it for granted that Bay, too, would live forever. I loved her and depended on her. My every childhood heartbreak sobbed into her warm sides, the scent of horse and tears a memory so deep that I smell it today. Bay passed away when I was a senior in high school. She had grown old while I grew up. Though times were good and there be other horses to ride on the ranch, none replaced her.

I don't remember a time when a horse wasn't a part of my life. They are so much a part of who I am that I even dream about them...sometimes dream that I am one of them. After college, while working in Kansas City, I sought them out; taking a part-time job at a stable just outside the city. With no horse of my own, I considered this the perfect opportunity. I satisfied my craving for contact with horses by cleaning stalls and exercising other people's animals. I rode away many home-sick hours in the fields and woods; all the while thinking what a wonderful joke it was that I was getting so much and getting paid to boot!

I married and could never quite make my city-born husband understand my attachment to horses. He considered my stable job beneath me and thought I spent too much time there. I quit to please him. It was the first and very last time I ever chose a man over a horse. In need of the extra income, I took on more hours at my full-time job. Trading my part-time job at the stable for over-time at my office proved to be a poor bargain indeed; especially when my husband left me because I was "too involved" with my work.

A visit to the home ranch turned into a move when I simply could not make myself go back to the city. I went just long enough to give my notice at the office; then I drove out and said good-bye to my equine and human friends at the stable before heading south towards home.

I didn't find a job and this was worrisome. I found solace in the horses; spending my days working with the two year olds and built myself a little business training for others. I took over running the whole place when Papa passed on. Several years later I remarried; this time to a man who loves horses as much as I do and together we have tried to keep the ranch as it was when I was little. But time, as always, has made this a hard thing to accomplish. I fought cancer for two and a half years and medical bills piled up. Using the knowledge I gained as a child, we "tightened up", sold cattle and horses and started to see daylight. Then his company came upon hard times and the feed bill for the horses came into direct competition with the food bill for the family.

So we did what we were taught long ago, we "tightened up" again. This time we cut it all to the bone and anything not totally necessary is being sold. I know in my heart it is the right thing to do, but it's hard to watch all you worked for go to the highest bidder. I tune out the sound of the auctioneer and focus on my Papa's words. "Starting over is a gift from God and always a good thing...it gives us something to look forward to."

Every memory has a horse in it, even the bad ones like today. I came out here thinking it would be easier if I didn't watch them sell; these creatures who I have bred and trained and poured my heart and soul into. This evening after everything is over and the last horse trailer has pulled out, I'll go to pasture where stands an old, big-hipped bay mare with one white sock. I'll lean with my face against her warm side, breathing deep the scent of memory and life. Tomorrow I'll go help the neighbors move their calves to the weaning pens. I'll ask my daughter to ride along while I tell the story of my Papa and starting over with one good horse who was the Last to Sell.

Debra Coppinger Hill

Stud?

He reminded me of Peter Ustinov,
  in "We're No Angels", with Bogie and Aldo Ray,
Each time he looked at me he repeated that one line…
  "Oh, it's that delicious little fat woman
              from yesterday!"

One thing that I don't tolerate,
  in children or a horse,
is the excessive use of one's teeth.
  It's the rule I strictly enforce.

But he would lurk behind the tool shed,
  laying in wait for his chance,
to take a hefty nip or two,
  from the seat of my ample pants,

He always took his nibbles,
  when my husband didn't see.
And like a fool, I let my husband,
  lull me into a false sense of security.

He said the Stud was full of spirit;
  I was just misunderstanding,
The horse only wanted my attention,
  he was only a tiny bit demanding.

And like a MORON, I listened,
  and I learned a lesson hard,
On why you trust your gut instincts,
  and never drop your guard.

A month went by, and he kept in check,
   his over-sized pearly-whites;
So confidently, I went about,
   my feeding chores one night.

That day, The Demon decided
   I'd make a tasty snack
And while I was unlocking the corral gate,
   he bit me...in the back.

I've been in a bad car wreck, and I've got two kids,
   I remember the pain of those nights;
But, I plumb forgot all about childbirth,
   from the searing pain of that one bite.

I'm not real sure what happened next,
   I just know I was totally un-composed,
'Cause the next thing I knew, I was standing there,
   with a handful of that Stud's nose.

I had my thumb and fingers in his nostrils,
   and I was squeezing with all my might
And Darlin', it had the desired effect,
   'cause his eyes were filled with fright.

I backed him across the corral,
   and right on into a stall.
I figured this was "my moment",
   so I began to squall...

I yelled at him like a wayward child.
   I brought his legitimacy into question,
And all the while I shook his head
   back and forth like a piston.

I told him he'd be sorry,
   that I'd get even good;
Then one more time, just for good measure,
   I disparaged his parenthood.

At this point, my husband is convinced,
   I went entirely insane;
But that's not true, or there'd have been
   a changing of that horse's name.

He would have become Alpo,
   or possibly Old Roy...
But I realized I had too much invested
   in the training of the old boy.

You see, I can be down-right reasonable,
   when given time to calm down;
Especially when I recall I make all the ranch decisions,
   when my husband is out of town.

So, now the Stud's a Gelding,
   and his whole attitude has changed;
'Cause that same afternoon I called the Vet.,
   and had his anatomy re-arranged.

Now on our place there are a few rules,
   but they're not that hard to follow;
Number one, is only make promises you will keep,
   don't speak words that are hollow.

Number two, is clean your room
   and put away your toys and pajamas.
And number three, is use your head,
   and never, for any reason, ever bite The Mama.

Debra Coppinger Hill

*"**Ain't it strange how thoughts of horses lost**
Mirror those of men passed on
And though they've gone to glory
Their spirit's never gone*

***Sometimes simple words seem best**
When final words we choose
He dern sure was a good one
He's the kind you hate to lose"*

Jay Snider
Rafter S Ranch, Oklahoma

Rancher's Rhapsody

The old mare stands in the edge of the trees
  that grow thick and tall by the creek;
As I cross the pasture to her hiding place,
  her posture says 'no need to speak'.

I know what she is up to,
  she tells me without a word;
She's grown tired and weary,
  of being the leader of the herd.

But this band of mares depends on her,
  to lead them through sudden storms;
Between the gates, past the trap,
  to the barn where they're safe and warm.

I place my hand upon her back,
  she nods and turns an ear;
Patiently she waits for my thoughts,
  seems satisfied that I'm near.

I look into her eyes and see
  the reflected image of my own worth;
And the heritage of our Ancestors,
  who established birthright to this earth.

Our family was ordained as stewards,
  long before fence-posts and wire;
Chosen as guardians of the land,
  blessed by God and tried by fire.

It is worth every single sacrifice
  we must make along the way;
For what they gave to make it ours,
  is a debt we must repay.

So I understand how she feels,
  I too am weary to the bone;
And sometimes I am certain,
  I can't face another day alone.

Duty-bound we accept responsibility;
  we will survive and endure;
Our destiny is in the hands of God,
  of this we can be sure.

So I lay my face against her neck
  and we lean into the wind;
The storms of life can't break us,
  though they may make us bend.

And bend we will, if that's what it takes
  to keep this piece of land;
Passed down through generations
  by those who took a stand.

The wind picks up and calls our names,
  and as it plays our timeless song,
We become part of the symphony,
  and our souls sing along.

As our hearts join in and beat in time,
  matching measure for measure,
We are gifted with more than worldly wealth,
  we become rich in spiritual treasure.

As the wind plays this Rancher's Rhapsody,
  we too are blessed and sanctified,
By the grace of the holy trinity
  of Grass and Water and Sky.

We put our faith in eternity together,
  in reverent prayer we bow our heads;
Two in agreement that God never fails,
  just like the scripture said.

Our spirits are reborn anew,
  as the rains come we are baptized;
Pilgrims in a divine cathedral,
  beneath the sacred open skies.

Drawing strength from one another,
  we know what must be done;
And we will be ever faithful
  to this life that is hard-won.

As receding clouds change the horizon,
  and the evening light grows dim,
We'll follow the wind back home,
  and lead the others in.

Debra Coppinger Hill

***"Give us one good horse
and one true, loyal friend,
And someone to remember us
at the very end."***

*Debra Coppinger Hill
4DH Ranch, Oklahoma*

COWBOY FAITH

It's being unashamed to pray,
to give thanks for this holy place;
It's a light in the heart that guides us,
as we live through and in God's grace.

*"The horse is prepared
against the day of battle:
but safety is of the Lord."*

Proverbs 21:31

Eagles in the Trees

I have stood in the Holy Place
   looking down on what God sees;
The mountains, grass and water
   and the Eagles in the trees.

I've listened to the sacred songs
   of Earth and Wind and Sky;
Opened my heart to it all
   and never questioned why.

Some call it Blessings
   Some call it Grace
Some call it Destiny
   to look upon God's face.

To earn the heart we're given
   we must freely give it away,
In the name of One Much Greater,
   we receive the gifts for which we pray.

To stand with His creations,
   to know we are His creations too,
Is a humbling revelation,
   through which our souls are renewed.

Come stand with me in the Holy Place
   look down on what God sees,
The mountains, grass and water
   and the Eagles in the trees.

Debra Coppinger Hill

The Sponsor

He's a rodeo cowboy, you might know his name,
Though he's yet to achieve much rodeo fame.

Five years on the circuit; spent most of that alone,
Then he got a sponsor, now he's never on his own.

He still has hard times, but his sponsor's got a plan,
And if he'll just follow, he'll be a better man.

This plan ain't just for rodeo; it changed his entire life,
He's just one more cowboy that rides for Jesus Christ.

This plan's not just for cowboys,
blue collar or business types.
See JESUS died for everyone;
He's the world's only light.

This young cowboy, most likely will ride for several years;
Then he'll sit back and remember the laughter and the tears.

How his sponsor was there down every single road,
And how he'd stop to thank him, for every bull he'd rode.

When this world has ended and he comes before the throne,
He don't need to worry 'bout where he'll call home.

When he stands up to be judged and JESUS looks at him,
He'll turn to the FATHER, and say, "*I sponsored him.*"

Robert Beene

Gone To The Mountains

Sometimes the mountains call so strongly
that I shall never know peace
Until I stand where Heaven begins
and the bonds of this life cease.

I do not wish to leave you;
I've not but words to leave behind.
I pray, when you read, you'll remember me,
as strong and loyal and kind.

I rode the trail for which I was called,
in my mind regrets have no place;
The adventure was there for the living,
my heart says I ran a good race.

So listen for me in the laughter
that comes easy among true friends;
In the sounds of men and horses
beneath a sky that has no end.

And know that I loved you one and all,
when you hear music or smell sage in the air;
Dance hard and live for the moment,
my spirit will always be there.

Celebrate life and love and the West;
be fearless and funny and bold;
Please take the time to finish
any stories that I've left untold.

Past the meadow where blue bonnets grow,
near the creek by the gate;
My horse stands rigged for an easy ride,
and I can no longer wait.

So tell them I've gone to the mountains,
to the land I loved and called my home;
That I ride with the wild Texas wind,
somewhere west of San Antone'.

Debra Coppinger Hill

**"It's hell to be a warrior
in a land that's growing tame;
The good times all are past and gone
and nothing is the same."**

TR Stephenson ~ Texas Outlaw Poet

* With love for TR, who gave me words and love and taught me how to be an outlaw. This poem was awarded the first TR Stephenson Memorial Cowboy Poetry Award by the San Antonio Poerty Fair.

A Cowboy's Request

I've heard the talk of golden streets
  and mansions on a hill;
For some I guess that's heaven,
  but God knows how I feel.

Me and my Christian friends are cowboys,
  and we'd never turn down God's grace;
But cities of gold ain't what we look to.
  See, we run a little different race.

We just want to serve the Lord;
  don't care much about money or jewels.
We live life different than most,
  though we still follow God's rules.

God wants us all to be happy.
  Christians don't have a sad heart.
He made us everyone different
  on purpose, right from the start.

So when I think of Heaven,
  my picture's quite different at best;
'Cause God knows us cowboys
  don't think like all the rest.

So here's a list of things
  that in Heaven I'd like to see;
But if I'm close to Jesus,
  that's all that matters to me.

If it's not too much trouble,
  a couple of good buckin' pens;
For Tommy, Justin, and Dustin,
  and all of my bull ridin' friends.

Some wide open prairies
  with grass boot-top tall;
With cattle to tend,
  and calves to brand each fall.

I'd sure like to see some good horses
  with Hancock in their veins;
The kind that'll stay with ya
  when you work all day on the plains.

I can't wait to ride up in Heaven,
  to make the first gather that fall;
With all of my friends and no fences to mend,
  I tell ya, we'll all have a ball.

Robert Beene

Echoes Of The Canyon

They say that she is crazy
  talking to the canyon;
Listening to the voices
  that echo from the rocks.
She knows that they are out there,
  the spirits of the Ancients,
And the moon, it makes her restless
  as it lights the path she walks.

The Storykeeper told her
  the water there flows crimson;
That the grass for the ponies,
  is lush and green and tall.
Among the stalks of sky-blue corn,
  medicine drums are calling;
The Old Ones shadow-dancing
  as the twilight starts to fall.

So she burns a little sage
  on a fire made of cedar;
Sending prayers out to them
  in a shower of sparks and smoke.
The flames bid her welcome
  into the Sacred Circle;
Her flute repeating softly,
  the promises that he spoke.

For her sacrifice and faith
  the Old Ones send a message;
A hawk dips down and beckons
  to follow ever high.
The path is steep and rocky,
  but she just keeps on climbing;
Waiting for the moment
  when she'll be allowed to fly.

One day, she simply disappeared.
  I like to think she found it;
That emerald endless valley
  where the Spirit Dancers dwell.
The only question left...
  do we deserve to go there?
I guess that's just a story
  that only time can tell.

So, will they think I'm crazy
  talking to the canyon?
Listening for her voice
  to echo from the stones...
Their thoughts do not concern me
  in my quest for the Great Forever;
Wandering the Crimson Canyon trails,
  searching for my home.

DebraCoppingerHill

*With love to TR...who set my feet back upon the good road.

My Kind Of Heaven

"Cowboys still ride the Open Range here,
Eagles still soar Wild and Free;
You can see where God's Hands,
have truly blessed this land,
Its Beauty cleansing the Spirit inside of Me."

Fred Hargrove
Cowboy, Singer, Songwriter

The Answer

Now I'm just a cowboy
  and ain't never said I was smart;
But it don't take a genius,
  to see this world's comin' apart.
Everyone's complainin'
  about crime, violence, and stuff;
They've a million different reasons,
  but the answers ain't that tough.

Just ten simple laws
  that have been around for ages;
God give 'em to Moses
  carved deep on stone pages.
I bet you've heard 'em before,
  maybe read 'em once or twice;
You ought to read 'em again,
  Friend, take my advice.

They are not suggestions!
  God said "This is My Law";
But this world has turned away,
  and taken quite a fall.
So, spend time with your Bible.
  Accept Jesus in your life.
Obey the Father's commandments,
  and he'll remove all strife.

He never said it'd be easy,
  but it's worth it, I believe.
And I'll meet you at the Eastern Gates,
  if Jesus you'll receive.

Robert Beene

Through The Dust

Waking to the sound of voices in the kitchen,
  the wind was sifting grit underneath my window sill.
Choking from the dust, I was driven from my covers,
  to the safety and the warmth, of my Mamma's arms.

Daddy reached across the table
  and touched my little hand,
Drinking down his coffee
  to that little bit of sand.
He said, "This storm's a bad one,
  it's gonna' howl all day."
Then he asked my Mamma,
  "Reckon God can hear us pray?"

> *She told him, "Prayer like dust, rises ever high,*
> *On wings of hope into the sky,*
> *Through darkness and despair,*
> *When we think no one is there,*
> *God hears our every prayer...through the dust."*

The dust boiled thick and heavy
  and covered up our dreams,
Invading nooks and crannies,
  filling all the seams.
As it whistled 'round the windows
  and sang a sad refrain,
To hold her fear at bay
  Mamma sighed a prayer for rain.

She wiped her brow and wet a sheet
  and hung it at the door.
I cleaned off the table,
  and then she swept the floor.

In a never-ending battle,
    she fought the cruel drought.
And her spirit never wavered,
    and I never heard her doubt.

> *That a prayer like dust, rises ever high,*
> *On wings of hope, into the sky.*
> *Through darkness and despair,*
> *When we think no one is there,*
> *God hears our every prayer...through the dust.*

Lost in the raging darkness
    Daddy struggled down the rope;
As the wind cut right through him,
    crushing all his hope.
He said, "Lord, I'm your servant
    but I just don't understand,
Why you let this endless wind
    blow away our land.

There's a place of milk and honey,
    further to the west.
Do we surrender now
    or stay and stand the test?
I try to comprehend.
    I don't mean to complain.
Lord, I'm looking for a sign,
    do we go or yet remain?"

> *And prayer, like dust rises ever high,*
> *On wings of hope into the sky.*
> *Through darkness and despair,*
> *When we think no one is there,*
> *God hears our every prayer...through the dust.*

When the dust quit blowing
   our lives were not the same.
We clasped our hands together,
   and thanked the Lord for rain.
Because dreams only die
   when they're buried for too long
And hopes and dreams are what sustain,
   our love and make it strong.

Beneath the dusty layers
   we found a brighter day.
We'd survived tribulation,
   hard times and dismay.
Renewed by God's own Mercy
   as He washed away the dust,
We leaned on each other,
   in Faith, Belief and Trust...

> *That a prayer said in faith only knows to fly,*
> *Up above the dust into a clear blue sky.*
> *It cuts through the darkness and despair,*
> *To the One who's always there,*
> *God hears our every prayer...through the dust...*

Debra Coppinger Hill & Jean Prescott
* Through The Dust appears on the Jean Prescott CD Tapestry of he West

"Water seeks its own level."

BJ Streeby ~ Cowgirl, Educator

How Long Will the Cowboy Last

Who will I be ten thousand years from now,
If someone digs up what's left
of this man who worked cows?

Will they think I'm a soldier or fighter of some kind,
From the scars of the countless
broken bones I'll leave behind?

Will they know I'm a puncher, who spent life on the range?
Will they know what a Cowboy is?
Is the world due so much change?

I guess it don't matter, for I know what I am today;
But will my descendants know
what a cowboy is in their day?

So when I die, place me in the ground.
Don't worry 'bout flowers
or friends gathered round.

Wrap me in a blanket, spurs on my booted feet,
a book by Will James,
and my rope rolled up neat.

Send me to meet the Lord with the tools of my trade.
I sure hope I'll need them
in the Heaven He's made.

If this world lasts long enough and the Cowboy way is lost,
Maybe when they dig me up
they'll remember what progress cost.

Robert Beene

Questions and Answers

Is it not the same air we breathe
blown around this world
by the winds of time?

Is it not the same ocean we sail
pulled around this world
by the currents of the past?

Is it not the same heartbeat we share
pulsing from deep within
this, our Mother Earth?

Is it not the same sky we stand beneath
as we are turned in the Great Circle
by the hands of God?

Caught up in a swirling whirlwind of change,
Around the world and across the range,
The energy of love will raise us from the dust,
To greet one another in faith and trust.

We will lift up our companions without fail,
Leave footprints of unity along the trail,
One Tribe together, in peace we stand,
Heart to heart and hand in hand.

It is the same air…
It is the same ocean…
It is the same heartbeat…
It is the same sky…
We are the Hands of God.

Debra Coppinger Hill

Top Hand

In his heart he is a Cowboy,
riding for the brand;
Doing what comes naturally
being a Top Hand.

In his mind's eye lies the prairie,
racing with the wind,
Where a great big world lays waiting,
just around the bend.

With waters pure as crystal,
and air just as clear,
He often stops to wonder,
just what he's doing *Here.*

Green pastures are what he longs for,
and a good horse by his side;
Saddled up and ready,
for the Long, Hard ride.

So, he gives up everything to go,
where no one's gone before;
He smiles, as if to say good-bye,
and silently slips out the door.

There will be no fancy speeches,
as he rides into the sun;
It's just some things are never quite finished,
and his work has just begun.

He's headed for the High Lonesome,
where he'll once more take a stand...
This Cowboy's heart is headed Home,
to ride for Heaven's Brand.

For Barry Scott Ross, Cowboy   *Debra Coppinger Hill*

❖❖❖❖❖❖❖

"A lifetime spent with horses,
teaches calmness to your soul;
A oneness with God and nature,
like things honest and old.
Grandpa always had that look
and my dear old daddy too;
In their eyes you could tell,
they were Cowboy through and through."

Tom Hanshew
Circle TK Ranch, Godley, Texas

Buffalo Dance

Rough, Untamed, Rush the draw
Primal energy, Passionate, Raw

Painted face, Feathered lance
So begins the Buffalo Dance

Race the Thunder over the hill
Take the world by sheer will

Free and Wild without care
Fearless screams Split the air

Call it Destiny...Call it Chance
Drums beat out the Buffalo Dance

Rise and Fall, the Liar's Moon
Death and Existence come too soon

Earth is made of Give and Take
Past and Future are at stake

Lightning strikes Evil askance
Spirits of Fire join the Buffalo Dance

Caution tossed to the Wind
Now is the place to begin

Turn the herd...Lead the pack
Valiant hearts blaze new tracks

Dreams are real, this is no trance
Life lived Full is the Buffalo Dance

Debra Coppinger Hill

One More Cowboy Day

Stir the campfire boys…Stir till it grows cold,
And the embers stop their glowin',
and the sparks quit poppin' bold.

As we come together and clasp our hands to pray,
Let's thank the Lord above for one more Cowboy day.

Stir the campfire boys…Stir till it's all out,
As we talk together,
of the things that life's about.

And as we laugh together and good memories are made,
We'll thank the Lord for one more Cowboy day.

Stir the campfire boys…As we fade into the night,
Secure in the knowledge,
that inside we hold the light.

And as the fire dies slowly, let it leave not a trace,
That here upon these rocks, stood a proud and noble race.

Stir the campfire boys…As we make one last request.
That each and every day,
we do our cowboy best.

And as the smoke drifts skyward to join the Milky Way,
We'll close our eyes and thank the Lord
for one more Cowboy day.

Debra Coppinger Hill

LESSONS LEARNED

**Once a Cowboy…Always a Cowboy,
no matter how long the day,
It's what we do, it's who we are
and we won't have it any other way.**

*"Folks, they call me Cowboy,
it's a name I wear with pride."*

*David W. King
Oklahoma Auctioneer,
Cowboy Poet, Singer & Songwriter*

Waiting

Sweat-stained Stetson,
On the wall,
Muddy boots,
In the hall,
Stand and wait,
Sometimes they call…Saddle-up and ride.

Spurs left hanging,
On a chair,
Saddle, oiled,
Over there,
Sit and wait,
With patient care…Saddle-up and ride.

Slow and quiet,
Horses walk,
Softly nicker,
Hear them talk,
Endure and wait,
But never mock…Saddle-up and ride.

Cowboy spirits,
In the night,
A haunting dance,
A lonesome sight,
Sway and wait,
For day's first light…Saddle-up and ride.

Saddle-up and ride,
Under stars and moonlight,
It's the only thing left that's right…Saddle-up and ride.

Debra Coppinger Hill

Ride to the Call of the West

Into the sun, at the end of day
  rides the Cowboy as he goes his way,
Across a chasm, seen in a dream
  the life of a Cowboy's forever it seems,
He is the balance in a dance
  in a time given over to chance.

Along the edge of a time drawn near
  when Cowboys and cattle are no longer here,
And for these things he's willing to fight,
  for freedom and honor, are privilege and right;
When the rest of the world is hopeless and cryin'
  he'll pull it all together or he'll die trying.

He fights the heat, the wind, and rain,
  if you don't know him you'll swear he's insane
He rides on a ridge of time and space
  some-how he feels out of place;
These words I give you please recall,
  the Cowboy who struggles, gives his all.

The life he lives is no mystery
  he's just out-lived his history;
The lesson I hope you understand
  the Cowboy is more than a part of this land;
His fight for things wild and free
  seals his fate and our destiny.

Ride to the call of the West my friend,
Ride to the lore of the brand, if you can,
Ride to the spirit of the Cowboy true,
Ride to his legend in this land.

Debra Coppinger Hill & Robert Beene

When the Glory's All Gone

He dreams of the days
when he was alive,
As he drives through the city
to his nine-to-five.

He remembers the circuit
he followed for years;
The bad bulls he rode,
the laughter and tears.

He recalls the women,
although not by name.
Their faces have faded,
just part of the game.

It wasn't the women
or the money he made;
He loved ridin' bulls,
but the memories fade.

They've lost track of him now,
since he's not on the road;
But 'round the pens they still talk
'bout bulls that he rode.

The guys at the factory
just don't want to hear,
About freedom and friends,
the bulls or the cheers.

They don't understand,
he knows they never will.
But he's been there, and man
it sure is a thrill.

When you step off a bull
and the crowd's on their feet,
It's some kind of feelin'
that's sure tough to beat.

The smell of the pens,
the sweat on your brow;
You pull off your hat
and wave to the crowd.

It don't last long,
Eight seconds is all;
And when it's all over,
it's a mighty long fall.

Robert Beene

**"My body and mind may have to be
in this office each day;
but my heart and soul will be
where there are horses and arena dust."**

Annie James
'She's Horse Crazy'

Common Sense, Men and Horses

We perched atop the corral,
  as he read the men and horses,
And he told me about common sense
  and it's amazing, magical forces.

We watched the men choose their mounts,
  some were firm, but kind;
While others used plain brute force,
  to make their horses mind.

He said, "Dealing with horses and people
  is a special kind of art;
If you watch 'em work, you will learn
  what is truly in a man's heart.

For though it once was common place,
  common sense ain't common any more
And many of the basic rules of life,
  some folks will choose to ignore.

The bad ones will make excuses,
  tell you the Old Cowboy ways have died;
But anyone with common sense
  will know that's a lie.

The truth is just as obvious
  as these fellows working the pens;
There will always be Cowboys
  as long as there are horses and men.

And just as it takes all kinds of horses,
  from renegades to leaders to make a herd;
There will also always be outlaws
  as well as men true to their word.

You see, a man who *can't,*
  will often bully his way through,
And how a man treats his horse
  is how he'll end up treating you.

But the man who *can*, simply will,
  he won't have to prove a thing.
He'll have the courage and the sand
  to face whatever life brings.

He never will desert you;
  even in the darkest hour
and he'll have the sense to know
  when to turn to a Higher Power.

The phrase, 'a soft hand with horses',
  applies to human beings too,
A man who is *one* with his horse
  will likewise be *one* with you.

You see, the decisions that we make
  should be rooted in our common sense.
Like horses, we should use our instincts,
  or be prepared to accept the consequence.

For no matter what we do in life,
  no matter where we roam,
We all are part of a family herd,
  and we can always come home."

So we watched 'em work for hours,
  as I hung on every word he had to say;
About life and love and horses;
  how God hears us when we pray.

I simply took it for granted
  that he would always be,
Sitting on that fence rail,
  talking and laughing with me.

Time makes changes as it passes by;
  I grew up and followed my star.
But in times of trouble I'd hear his voice,
  saying "Remember who's child you are."

He taught me to read the world
  though I didn't know it at the time.
I learned about strength and self-respect;
  how to recognize the best in mankind.

Oh, I made mistakes, but have no regrets,
  for each is valuable in its own way.
Combined with his words and an education,
  they comprise who I am today.

And nothing ever really gets me down,
   because of these things I can be sure;
That home is where the heart is,
   and that love will forever endure.

So I honor this Cowboy philosopher,
   who taught me to follow my heart's voice;
To see things exactly for what they are
   and that happiness is a choice.

I've come to realize all those things I learned,
   from books and college courses,
Will never hold a candle to his lessons,
   on Common Sense, and Men and Horses.

Debra Coppinger Hill

**"*Everything I know about horses and men
I learned from my Grand-daddy.
Life is too short to put up with
bad-tempered beings of either species.*"**

*Debra Coppinger Hill
4DH Ranch*

The Seed

He was a cowboy back in the days of old,
When bein' a puncher meant you were awful bold.
Back before fences, squeeze chutes and such;
When a higher education just didn't mean much.

When a man wasn't judged by a paper on the wall,
But by the work he did and how he took a fall.
He used to tell me back when I was a kid,
'Bout the old days and all the things he did.

"Son it was great. Regrets, I ain't got a one.
Just bein' a cowboy's the best thing under the sun."
He told of long drives, the cowboys he'd knowed;
Of cagey old cows, and the broncs they had rode.

He'd planted a seed; it was more than a dream.
So I started cowboyin' at the age of sixteen.
I know he glorified it some and it's hard to explain;
The cold, the snow, the bite of the wind and rain.

I've been cowboyin' now for about ten years,
And I'll tell ya fer sure, there ain't been no tears.

Robert Beene

**"The only way to pay for your raisin',
is to raise one of your own."**

Monte Gaylord ~ GaylordQuarterHorses.com

Barn Therapy

I go hide out in the barn sometimes,
just to take a small vacation,
From the telephone, the fax machine,
and my all too close relations.

Hiding out in the barn,
sets my mind at ease.
I watch the chickens, sit on the hay,
and listen to the breeze.

I learn a lot just sitting there,
observing the things I see,
And hiding out in the barn,
is cheaper than therapy.

I can psycho-analyze my id,
get in touch with my inner self;
Meditate and mediate,
and improve my mental health.

There are times,
(I'm not ashamed to say),
I go hide out there,
for the better part of the day.

There's much to be said,
for routinely hiding-out;
I come to understand,
what my life is all about.

I leave the barn,
refreshed and renewed,
My problems are minimal,
and my tensions subdued.

I know that I am lucky,
to have found the key,
To putting my world in order,
and finding perfect tranquility.

So if you come looking for me,
I'll be where simple things hold real charm;
Getting a dose of therapy,
hiding-out, in the barn.

Debra Coppinger Hill

Define Hobby

The IRS has once again challenged my choice of occupation. Though I've ranched thirty years, submit all required paper work and NEVER cheat on my taxes; I must periodically prove I'm really a *Rancher*. They insist raising livestock is a potential 'hobby' and send volumes of documents designed to strike fear in my heart and strain the back of our postman.

Looking up the definition of 'hobby' I found this:

hob-by *n*. An activity or interest undertaken for fun or pleasure during one's leisure time.

I'm convinced my livelihood isn't a 'hobby'. No one in their right mind would undertake my job as a 'hobby'. No sane person in search of *fun* would get up repeatedly at night to slog through the cold and wet to check expectant mares. No one seeking *pleasure* would lie on their stomach in muddy amniotic fluid with their arm up a cow turning a twisted calf. Stacking hay in 105 degree weather isn't advertised at any resort as a *leisure* activity. No travel agent books vacations featuring sleep deprivation during foaling and calving seasons with a probability of being kicked, bitten, run over or head-butted. If this is what they define as *fun*, please explain it to me.

Then why would anyone in their right mind do this for a living? *Heritage*; we ranch because we're tied to the land through countless generations who desired independence. It's our culture, our birthright, our passion; the *fun* is the satisfaction of upholding tradition. We contribute to the economy, support local schools and the general welfare of the United States by being good citizens. We stay self-employed, employ others and pay our taxes on time. We

If that weren't bad enough
  the boss looked at me and grinned;
"I guess it'd be okay
  if you ride with your new friend"
I dang near drew my pay.
  there's other range to ride
And draggin' yearlings to the fire
  a man can lose some hide.

The boss knew I was mad
  but he sat and rolled a smoke;
"I know what's on your mind,
  you think this is all a joke.
 You think this kid's a waste
  and it might be that your right,
But before you write him off
  let's see if he's got some fight."

So we caught up the little bay
  he borrowed a saddle, of course,
And we all gathered round to see
  if this kid could ride a horse.
As we saddled up the pony,
  his mouth it didn't stop;
I could tell by the way he talked
  he thought I was dumb as a rock.

He was tryin to impress us
  with all the things he knew;
I just smiled, drew up the cinch
  and said, "this pony's for you".
Well I held the horse's head
  as he climbed up in the saddle;
Looked like a man headed upstream
  in a boat without a paddle.

Now Bay weren't bad to buck,
  but the kid got him confused;
He pulled both reins and kicked him;
  Bay figured he's bein' abused.
He finally slacked up on the reins
  and ole bay took off on a run,
And jumped clean out from under him,
  he hit the ground like a ton.

He weren't really hurt,
  'cept maybe his pride,
But he just sat there cryin'
  like he's about to die.
He finally got to his feet
And he's sure fightin' mad,
"You done that on purpose,
  you knew that horse was bad."

I walked to ole Bay,
  picked the reins up off the ground,
Stepped into the saddle
  and started ridin him around.
We loped over to the kid
  and I stepped out of the kack;
Then handed the reins to him,
  he looks at 'em an hands 'em back.

A man that can't ride ain't much good,
  but the boss said "don't give up yet",
So we put him on the ground crew,
  but weren't nobody taken bets.
We were draggin' 'em to the fire;
  brandin', vaccinatin' and such;
Even when not tangled in the ropes
  he still wasn't worth very much.

He couldn't throw a calf,
  they kept slippin' through his hands;
Then the boss hollered out
  see if he can set a brand.
So we headed for the fire
  when I stops to light a smoke,
Then heard him screech and holler
  I looked and thought, 'what a dope!'

Now an iron's got two ends,
  one to hold, and one not.
I know it's hard to believe
  but he picked the end that's hot.
The boys all come a runnin',
  but the burn weren't all that bad;
Then he looks over at the boss
  and says "I gave it all I had."

"This job ain't what I thought
  ya'll know I'm way too smart,
To be here punchin cows,
  just isn't in my heart."
So he headed for his car,
  lookin down his nose at us;
Like we were nothin' better
  than a little speck of dust.

When I hollered out
  he stopped dead in his tracks,
He knew what I said
  was surely based in facts.
"Son, you may be plenty smart
  with all that high-dollar knowledge
But you failed Cowboyology
  at a Working Cowboy's College."

Robert Beene

Dirt Road

The traffic flies by at a fast-paced clip;
on a warm spring day it's a nice little trip.
The county came in and smoothed out the road,
past the porch where we sat and learned of *The code*.

In my mind I still see him though he is long gone,
and I still hear the words to his old Cowboy songs.
He spoke of the cow trails and called them by name;
said the dust all around us was one and the same.

He gave us the stories of the days that were past.
We looked to the future and swore we'd make them last.
We rode our stick ponies and rounded up strays,
and we knew we'd be Cowboys for all of our days.

The buildings stand empty, a testimony to time;
but they're filled with the dreams that I still call mine.
You can blacktop a road, but they'll always be there,
those dust covered memories that hang in the air.

They've paved the dirt road that rolls by the farm,
where we laughed & played Cowboy in the fields and barn.
We learned where we came from, who we could be;
and the dust of that dirt road, is still part of me.

Debra Coppinger Hill

Mechanized Ranches

He said that cowboyn' was a thing of the past,
That modern techniques were just as fast.
Less stress on the cattle or that's what he thought;
But I don't see a squeeze chute as an easy way to get caught.

He's moved a hundred head a mile or even more,
To doctor one calf that was getting' poor.
I tried to explain that a rope was so much fitter;
I'd slip in, rope him easy like and doctor that poor critter.

"Naw, that's too much stress. We'll take'm to the pens."
So we point' for the squeeze chute and pushed 'em all in.
Now all this modern stuff has surely raised a fuss;
But some of it, I must agree, has helped a lot of us.

Ivomec was sent from God, of this I have no doubt.
And the cowman will agree, it's helped to win the bout.
Though they teach in Ag., the use of this mechanical rack;
It never willl replace the Cowboy, his rope and his kack.

Robert Beene

This Ain't the Ritz

It's a little local place, it doesn't even have an official name;
folks around here just call it *The Diner*. Yesterday a tourist
happened in about 10:15 am and asked for breakfast. This
posed no problem as they serve breakfast till 10:30. He
ordered and received his coffee and his meal, of which he ate
every bite. But when they brought him the bill and asked
how his meal was he proceeded to inform the owner (Jim) of
his discontent. "The food was good, but my waitress
appeared to have manure on her cowboy boots and it entirely
ruined my appetite. This would never happen at the
restaurants I go to in New York."

Jim is a nice guy. He runs a nice small town café with good
food and good people serving it. The scolding he gave the
complainer went on of quite awhile. It was eloquent and I
smiled through the whole thing. After the tourist left, Jim
glanced at me and said, "There you go…write a poem about
that." Can do, Jim.

The tourist said the waitress had manure on her boots,
    that the very sight of it had ruined his delicate appetite;
And though he'd eaten every scrap of food on his plate,
    he felt the need to make a complaint about the sight.

"In New York, one would never see such a thing,
    One's senses would never be so offended."
He had the whole diner's rapt attention,
    before his haughty complaining was ended.

Soaking it in, owner Jim, leaned on the counter and said,
    "That gal fed cows for three hours before coming to work,
She does an 9 hour shift, then works past dark on the farm,
    so how dare you look down on her and smirk.

She raises three kids, while her husband's in Iraq,
  and she don't whine, she just does what she should,
And I wouldn't reprimand her for manure on her boots,
  though I'd give you a good shake if I could.

She works hard for her money, and don't ask for help,
  she's a good waitress, and she's considerate and sweet.
So what if she has manure on the souls of her boots…
  it ain't like she's serving you with her feet.

So feel free to go someplace in New York for your meals,
  where the staff's choice of footwear won't give you fits;
Because all you'll get here is good food and a smile;
  face it Mister, this ain't the Ritz.

But if it was then I'd be the head maître d',
  and I'd bounce you out on your snobby ear.
So it's my recommendation you move on,
  because you ain't much welcome in here."

"Your breakfast is free," said Jim to the tourist,
  "and thanks to that gal's husband, so are we;
You've had your say so and I've had mine,
  that's how it works in the Land of the Free."

As the tourist fumed out of the diner,
  a satisfied smile came across Jim's lips,
And because the tourist hadn't left one,
  he went to the table and laid down a tip.

Then every customer in the diner that morning,
  walked over and did the very same thing,
Tokens of thanks to the girl with manure on her boots,
  and her husband's sacrifice to preserve Freedom's ring.

Debra Coppinger Hill

*"I bought them when I was young
the leather was fresh and new,
I've worn them my whole life,
on the back of many a Cayuse.*

*Now they're dried and cracked,
but their hide is as tough as mine;
They may be old and worn,
but they still suit me fine."*

*David King
Cross Bar K Ranch, Oklahoma*

A Leather Bound Hero

He was a cowboy all of his life
  and he could remember the days of the drive.
He was thirteen years old when he took his first job
  wranglin' for Goodnight on a long dusty drive.

He rode into history though few knew his name.
  A leather bound hero not lookin' for fame.
He lived in the time before the land grew tame
  He saddles his pony and rides the range.

He lived through the days on the range 'neath the stars
  and in to the age of fences and cars.
Though cowboyin' changed he tried to hold on,
  to the old days and old ways he knew soon would be gone

He rode into history though few knew his name.
  A leather bound hero not lookin' for fame.
He lived in the time before the land grew tame.
  He'd saddle his pony, another day on the range

He told me one time that he didn't belong
  in a world with no freedom, how'd it all go so wrong;
With asphalt and fences they cut up the range
  and brought a way of life that to him was so strange.

Then he rode into history though few knew his name.
  A leather bound hero not lookin' for fame.
He lived past his time, the land has grown tame.
  We unsaddled his pony, it's the end of the game.

Robert Beene

Long Shadow Days

Tuff pads across the hot gravel at the end of the drive, his shadow following long and lean. He is old this dog. I do not say "this dog of mine", for he is independent; owns me more than I own him. No longer youthful, he has long ago given up chasing rabbits, so Mr. Bunny sits among the nasturtiums and gobbles the bright blossoms.

At the corner of the garden Tuff pauses to drink from the old turkey roasting pan left just where the leaky faucet can drip fresh water all day. I could fix it, make it like new and save on the water bill; but then who would make sure he has a cool drink when I am away? My day job is in town now; an office position taken when the horse market went thin and kept 'just in case'.

Tuff used to lie at my feet where-ever I was. His rhythmic panting setting the pace as I went about my chores. We were constant and consistent comrades and I missed him once the job started. I snuck him to work once when I thought the Boss would be gone all day. Tuff lay beneath my desk, his head on the toe of my boot, content like the old days to just be touching me. As co-conspirators we'd have gotten away with it too, if the Boss and his son hadn't showed up late in the afternoon.

Tuff could ignore the Boss, but he doesn't like the son, so he stuck his head out and growled real low. I made the excuse that I had to take him to the veterinarian immediately after work and needed to save gas and time by not backtracking home. The Boss said it was ok just this once and petted Tuff, while his son said he never could understand why dogs don't like him much. I allowed that some old dogs are just that way sometimes and they left and went on about their business. Tuff and me, we know the truth and agree that some folks just deserve growling at.

I watch as Tuff settles on his rug on the side porch and stares off towards the east pasture where the cows and calves used to stand in the shade. Sometimes I think he misses them and that he is reflecting on the old days, when he was a real jaw-snappin' cow-dog with the world by the tail. Maybe it's just me, sliding into old memories of when I was just as young and bullet proof.

The sun shifts and I realize it is getting late. I drive on down from the top of the hill where I have been watching and stop at the gate to pick up the mail. Tuff's ears go up and he races across the yard and circles the fence to meet me. I open the truck door and he jumps up and wiggles in between me and the door. As I shut the door he sticks his left front leg and head out the window. To anyone coming along our road it looks like he is driving; our little joke on passers-by.

I park by the chutes and like a young pup Tuff bounds out of the truck, barrels full speed across the yard and barks at the rabbit in the flower bed. I smile at his attempt to fool me into believing he stays on guard all day. I praise him, call him 'good dawg' and laugh as he picks up his rug and shakes it.

He dashes a few feet ahead of me as we follow a nightly routine of walking to the barn to feed the horses. His shadow and mine mix together and form a creature of mythological proportion. Looking back to where I lag behind, he pauses and waits for me. I envy his patience, his contentment with his life as it is; find comfort in his unconditional companionship. I catch up and we walk on, two shadows before us, touching now and then in that familiar way of kindred spirits.

I like to think that the road to Heaven's gate is like this; an easy walk along a frequented path with a good, trusted friend. In these long-shadow days it is comforting to know there is someone there who loves us for no other reason than we are consistently there. As evening falls and the shadows stretch out far ahead of us I realize something. They do not show age. They are as we were. And with Tuff by my side, that is enough.

Debra Coppinger Hill • Riding Drag

Buffalo Grass

The round bales stand, heavy and grand,
  it's been a good year for hay.
Up the hill I walk, to sit on my rock,
  as master of all I survey.

It occurs to me, this used to be,
  part of the open plain;
Before you and me, before cattle was king,
  the royal Buffalo reigned.

Clouds edged with light, day eases to night,
  dusk plays tricks with my eyes;
Into visions I drift, shapes start to shift,
  Night-hawks sing a lullabye.

The moon rises low, shadows come and go,
  I see shaggy beasts in the haze.
They come as I sleep, give me knowledge to keep,
  I watch them content as they graze.

They ramble on in, I call them kin,
  I awake to find them not there;
But it's not been a dream, I still feel the steam,
  of their sacred breath in the air.

The water still flows. The wind still blows.
  The bluestem waves tall and green.
And I see them each night, when the moon is just right,
  the Buffalo of my dreams.

I breathe a prayer, while I'm standing there
  and hope it's not too late;
To save the earth, for what it's worth,
  or we'll suffer the very same fate.

I'll heed their call…Pray for us all,
  ask God "Where do we go?"
When the moon is pale, I'll stand near the bales,
and pretend…they're Buffalo.

Debra Coppinger Hill

Take Me Back to the West

Take me back to the West
to a time when we did ride;
In perfect syncopation,
man and horse in flawless stride.

Take me back to the West
to the prairie open and free;
To buffalo, in grass belly tall,
as far as the eye can see.

Take me back to the West,
let me breathe clean mountain air;
Let me see the azure sky
as if I'm standing there.

Take me back to the West
to herds of horses fat and slick;
To rolling seas of bluestem
no plow has yet to nick.

Take me back to the West
through poetry and song;
Give me that peaceful stillness
for which my soul does long.

Take me back to the West
to that place that holds my heart;
Tell me, always I will stay
and from it, never part.

Debra Coppinger Hill

❖❖❖❖❖❖❖

*"Oftentimes my body rejects the flatlands
and I can only find peace in the beauty
of the mountains or high plains."*

*Angela Beene
Photographer of the American West*

The Pictures We Paint

He clocks in each morning and opens his toolbox,
to the pictures taped to the lid;
From an old magazine, they serve to remind him
of places he loved as a kid.

One of a Cowboy draggin' an ole' steer,
up to the hot branding iron;
Another of friends gathered up in the evening,
swappin' tales 'round a warm cookin' fire.

And in his mind he's up ridin' high in the mountains,
and down in the valley below,
Getting lost in the dream that he'd like to find,
in the pictures he paints in his mind.

She works in an office surrounded by windows,
twenty-five floors from the ground;
Caught up in the rat race of the 9 to 5 world,
she dreams of the sweet prairie sounds.

And she longs for the feel of the soft saddle leather,
that her office chair can't provide.
The horse in a painting carries her away
and across the wide prairie she rides.

And in her mind she's up ridin' high in the mountains,
and down in the valley below,
Getting lost in the dream that she'd like to find,
in the pictures she paints in her mind.

We get lost in the pictures we hang on the walls,
of the places we hold in our hearts,
And live out our lives in day-dream pieces,
forgetting that life is an art.

Through the coulies and draws of our minds we go ridin',
to the places that we wish to be;
Then the real world around us, completely surrounds us,
with the day to day lives that we lead.

But in our minds we're ridin' up high in the mountains,
and down in the valley below,
Getting lost in the dreams that we'd like to find,
in the pictures we paint in our minds.

David King ♦ Debra Coppinger Hill ♦ Robert Beene.

Once a Cowboy...

Once a Cowboy...Always a Cowboy,
It's born into the blood,
It takes a man's true measure,
through rain-storm, wind and flood.

It knows no age or gender,
you receive just what you earn,
By stepping up, taking hold of the reins,
and never complaining about your turn.

It's a sacred eternal connection,
as man and horse meet eye to eye,
And our spirits experience freedom,
as we break loose and fly.

It's being unashamed to pray,
to give thanks for this holy place;
It's a light in the heart that guides us,
as we live through and in God's grace,

Once a Cowboy...Always a Cowboy,
no matter how long the day,
It's what we do, it's who we are
and we won't have it any other way.

Debra Coppinger Hill

Many Thanks

We wondered if there were too many pages dedicated to acknowledgements; but we believe you can never be too thankful. So, dear reader, please bear with us as we say thank you to all those who have extended a helping hand along the trail.

- Mr. Moyer of the Moyer Ranch, Kansas for allowing us the privilege of participating in the 2007 roundup and for your gracious hospitality that made many of the photographs in this book possible.
- To the Cowboys and Cowgirls of all ages who did an exceptional job at the Moyer Roundup and for allowing our photographer access to great moments.
- To our co-writers who took our poems and made them into music, contributed words when we were stuck; who have shared their time, talent and quotes. Thanks, David W. King, Jean Prescott, Jen D. Enise, Jon Messenger and Devon Dawson, Tom Hanshew, Tim Graham, Annie James, Emily Richardson, BJ Streeby, Jeff Streeby, Leigh Ann Matthews, Jay Snider, Duffy Moore, Monte Gaylord and Fred Hargrove. Cowboys & Cowgirls one and all!
- Leigh Ann Matthews for including us in her wonderful publication *The Southwest Horse Trader*.
- Trey & Pam Allen for their friendship and for keeping a bucket in the freezer for Angela.
- The guys at EC Printing for being professional and for teaching us how to make things right.
- Deborah Collins for her encouragement, her help in finding EC Printing and for teaching us about *proper tea*, scones and clotted cream.
- Jessica Carpenter and the crew at Trade West.
- And to Bessie and Larry Lawrence for allowing Debra time, equipment and *proper tea* parties.

From Debra

It is my privilege to have wonderful family, friends, teachers and mentors. I would like to acknowledge the following for their contributions to my life.

- Mrs. Beth Young and Dr. Billie Ross: Teachers in the truest sense of the word.
- My family for love and support, and for sitting at performances in 105 degree parking lots. You are the greatest parents, brother, sister-in-law, nephew, grand-parents, aunts, uncles and cousins, etc.!
- True Friends having earned the title "Friemly": friends who are family. You know who you are.
- My trail partners Robert and Angela for True Friendship and hard work that made this all possible.
- Mr. Beener for allowing me to perform at WOCPG.
- Teresa for 40+ years of soul sharing and laughter.
- Jimmie Darlene for standing fire watch with me all night in the hay field and for letting us borrow Bob.
- Cherished Kindred Spirit Jeannie Sutton Hogue whose research saved me from cancer and who always told the truth. Though she now rides in Glory, she remains a vibrant force and an inspiring example. (Tell Rick thanks for the pennies.)
- My daughter Dara for helping keep the horses and me cared for. You are my pride and joy. To my son Dalan and daughter-in-law Lendsey, for your help and for giving me my grandson Derrick. I am proud of you all. To my husband David, for allowing me the gift of being able to live the life others just get to dream about. Thanks for understanding the insanity of *being a writer* and not having me committed.
- God, for his Son and for giving me all of the above.

I love you all. Wado! *Debra Coppinger Hill*

Debra Coppinger Hill

Cherokee Native Oklahoman, Debra Coppinger Hill manages the family's 4DH Ranch where they raise registered Cutting and Ranch Work horses. As a Cowboy Poet, columnist, song writer and storyteller, she writes about what she knows best: Cowboys, Cowgirls, Horses and the Land. Her writing ranges from serious to inspirational to thoughtful and humorous.

Debra holds an *Academy of Western Artists Will Rogers Award for Excellence in Cowboy Poetry*. She has performed and taught Cowboy and Western poetry across North America and in Ireland at the *Gerard Manley Hopkins Institute* to international students. She was honored by Hopkins with a showing of her Cherokee Bead Art.

Debra and her Oklahoma Cowboy Poet Friends performed *Cowboy Poetry on the floor of the House of Representatives of the State of Oklahoma* and received Citations from the State for their efforts in preserving this form of literature. She holds the honor of being the recipient of the very first *TR Stephenson Memorial Cowboy Poetry Award* from the San Antonio Poetry Fair.

She is published in collections by WestWord Press, Gibbs-Smith, Southwest Whispers, and Wild Buckaroo Press and appeared in *American Cowboy* magazine. Her chapbook & CD *Common Sense, Men and Horses* and her CDs of Cowboy Poetry received top five & top ten nominations respectively from the AWA and from the Western Poets Circle. Debra has been featured in *USA Weekend* and holds the honor of being the *Resident Poet of Cowboys-n-Cowgirls.com* and *AlwaysCowboy.com*.

Debra's syndicated column *Riding Drag* features Western poetry and vignette style stories and is published in the Morris Trade West Publications, Oklahoma's premiere equine paper *Southwest Horse Trader* and is syndicated to additional rural papers across the United States.

Debra is a federal and tribal registered Cherokee and writes Native American poetry. Her Cherokee art and beadwork is in private collections around the world.

Her Cowboy Poetry and columns are structured in several groupings that are educational in nature. She and her partners have presentations that can be tailored to fit specific school curriculums. They have a presentation with the Buckaroo Puppets that carries an anti-alcohol and anti-drug message. She and Robert and Angela Beene head the *Cowboys for Western Literature in the Libraries Project* which helps small rural libraries, schools and universities to acquire collections of Cowboy Poetry.

Debra owns and operates Old Yellow Slicker Productions. She and her friends at Lazy B Productions are happy to help groups and individuals produce a Western Event. They can tailor a show to fit any budget, from a one man show to a full festival.

For Debra's Poetry go to: www.oldyellowslicker.com
For her Column *Riding Drag* go to: www.ridingdrag.com
For more go to: www.cowboys-n-cowgirls.com

CONTACT: Old Yellow Slicker Productions
PO Box 348 ~ Chelsea, Oklahoma 74016 ~ 918-789-5288
Email: oldyellowslicker@yahoo.com

From Robert

Nobody gets through life on their own, so there are a lot of people to blame for how I turned out.

First to my parents: Thanks for allowing me to grow up horseback and for giving me the freedom to follow my dream of being a cowboy.

To all the cowboys I've worked with thanks for the lessons, the friendship, and the laughs. Not to mention the stories ya'll gave me to write about.

To my wife, well there's just too much to write about. Thanks for everything.

Robert Beene

Robert Beene

Robert Beene was born and raised in Oklahoma. He began riding bulls in rodeos at the age of sixteen and continued to ride for the next seventeen years. Robert worked on several ranches in Oklahoma and Nebraska before starting his career as a Farrier. He continues this occupation today with clients at ranches and stables across the state of Oklahoma. In addition he holds a degree in Biology from Southeastern State University.

Robert writes cowboy poetry and songs that are inspired by his life's events. He performs his rhyme and lyrics at various cowboy poetry gatherings, rodeos, weddings, private parties and corporate events.

He and his wife Angela hosted the, "Western Oklahoma Cowboy Poetry Gathering". Originally held the first weekend each November at Red Rock Canyon State Park in Oklahoma this gathering features top names in the world of Cowboy Poetry and Music. Their show has featured Award winning artists such as Debra Coppinger Hill, Jay Snider, Tim Graham and Trey Allen.

Robert and his Oklahoma Cowboy Poet Friends performed Cowboy Poetry on the floor of the *House of Representatives of the State of Oklahoma* this year and received Citations from the State for their efforts in preserving this form of literature.

Robert's poetry has been published in collections by *WestWord Press*, *The Christian Ranchman*, award winning collaboration of the world's top Cowboy Poets *The Big Roundup* and *American Western Magazine*. His poems are featured on *Cowboys-n-Cowgirls.com*. In addition, his songs and poetry have been recorded by himself and various Western singers and are heard on radio stations throughout the United States and Australia.

Robert is a proud member of Cowboys for Christ and the Academy of Western Artists. He has been nominated for the AWA's Rising Star, Male Cowboy Poet, and Cowboy Poetry album awards. Robert also works with local schools to help teach children Western heritage and to promote cowboy poetry to today's youth. He, Angela and Debra Hill head the *Cowboys for Western Literature in the Libraries Project* which helps small rural libraries, schools and universities to acquire collections of Cowboy Poetry.

Robert's tape/CD is available for purchase. It contains 11 cowboy poems and 3 songs that are all his original work. *Cowboyology* holds nominations from the AWA. Rafter S Timed Event President Jay Snider says "*Cowboyology* will give you insight into the heart and soul of a true cowboy."

Robert and Angela are the owners of Lazy B Productions. They and their associates at Old Yellow Slicker are happy to help groups and individuals produce a Western Event. They can tailor a show to fit any budget, from a one man show to a full festival.

Sound clips are available at the bottom of this web page. www.cowboys-n-cowgirls.com/Robert_Beene.html

Contact Robert at 405-923-0390
Email: lazybproductions@yahoo.com

From Angela

First and foremost, I would like to thank God. I have had both good times and truly bad times in my life, but He has always been there with me. I am also grateful that He showed me the thing that I am great at and that I love to do, photography, and allowed me to turn it into a career.

I would also like to thank my family for their constant love and support, despite my lunacy. My mother has always been the level-head that sets me straight when I begin to stray too far. My father is the one who taught me life is too short to be unhappy. He is also the voice in my head telling me that I can achieve anything. My sister has been an unwavering friend, confidant, and supporter of anything and everything I do (although she occasionally will slip an "I told you so" into the conversation).

Thank you to my son, Peyton, for keeping the child in me alive and kicking. You are truly my most frustrating and rewarding accomplishment! And thank you Dusty for reminding me that an 11 year-old can be smarter than I am, and that it's okay to jump on the bed as long as we call it "dancing".

And last but not least, thank you to my husband Robert. I don't really know what to say other than...you were my missing piece. You are my true love, my inspiration, and my best friend. Thank you for tolerating me as long as you have without *too many* attempted homicides.

I would not be here if it weren't for each and every one of you. I love you all!

Angela Beene

Angela Beene

Angela Beene was born, raised and remains a native Oklahoman. Growing up in Oklahoma, it's hard to not be exposed to the western lifestyle...at least in part. Then by marrying a true cowboy, she compounded her love and interest of this lifestyle and the people that live it everyday.

In her photographic journeys, she has captured everything from the birth and death of horses and the rounding-up, pushing, and shipping of cattle to ranch rodeos and cowboy gatherings. She has been a part the cowboy life long enough to know how to truly capture its essence in photos.

Angela received Professional Photography training from the New York Institute of Photography. She is the owner ABC Photography, which specializes in weddings, corporate and portrait work. Her photography has been published in textbooks, magazines, CD covers, reading books and several other mediums.

She has photographed many well-known Oklahomans such as Governor Brad Henry, attorney Stephen Jones, former OU head-coach Barry Switzer, and Attorney General Drew Edmondson. She's also had the pleasure of photographing some Oklahomans who are known only as *good ole' boys*, as well as many of the top Cowboy and Cowgirl Poets and Singers performing today.

Angela holds a position on the Board of Directors for Operation: Love Reunited (OpLove). OpLove is a non-profit organization of professional photographers who lend their creative energies to raising the morale of our men and women in uniform by donating their time and services. It is all made possible by artists who want to give something back to those who make the United States what it is, and who ask for nothing in return – but for these men and women to come home safely. For more information on OpLove, visit: www.oplove.org.

For Angela's cowboy photography, visit: www.angelabeene.com
For her other photography work, visit: www.abcphotography.net

CONTACT: Angela Beene at (405) 923-0290
420 SW 2nd Street ~ Jones, OK 73049
Email: info@angelabeene.com

Photographs

Cover photograph and all photographs in this publication copyright ©Angela Beene with the exception of photos on pages 31 and 79 which are copyright ©Debra Coppinger Hill and Debra's biography photo by ©Jeff Streeby, taken at Inis Mor, Aran Islands, Ireland. No reprints or usage of these images in any media without written permission of the photographer. Individual copyrights apply.

We Recommend:

WestWord Press
www.westwordpress.com
•

American Cowboy Company
www.AmericanCowboyCompany.com
For Books by WestWord Press, Cowboy Poetry & Music CDs,
Western Photograph, Arts and Crafts.
•

Old Yellow Slicker Productions ~ *www.oldyellowslicker.com*
•

4DH Ranch – Cutting and Ranch Work Horses
www.4dhranch.com
•

Lazy B Productions ~ *www.lazybproduction.com*
•

AngelaBeene.com ~ ABCPhotography.net
Western Photography, Prints & Art: *www.AngelaBeene.com/store*
•

For Western Image Clothing and Gift Items:
AlwaysCowboy.com
or www.cafepress.com/AlwaysCowboy
•

Cowboys-n-Cowgirls.com ~ TheCowboyCompany.com
•

Tom Hanshew
www.cowboys-n-cowgirls.com/TomHanshew_Bio.html
•

TimGrahamCowboyMusic.com
•

Southwest Horse Trader ~ *www.swhorse-ok.com*
•

Debra's Column: ***www.RidingDrag.com***
or www.TradeWestOnline.com
•

JaySnider.net
•

GaylordQuarterHorses.com
•

HeartlandAngel.com